ONE ON ONE

THE BEST WOMEN'S
MONOLOGUES

FOR THE 21ST CENTURY

ONE ON ONE

THE BEST WOMEN'S MONOLOGUES

FOR THE 21ST CENTURY

EDITED BY
JOYCE E. HENRY
REBECCA DUNN JAROFF
BOB SHUMAN

APPLAUSE THEATRE & CINEMA BOOKS
An Imprint of Hal Leonard Corporation
New York

Published in 2007 by
Applause Theatre and Cinema Books
An imprint of Hal Leonard Performing Arts Publishing Group
19 West 21st Street, New York, NY 10010

Printed in the United States of America

Book design by Kristina Rolander

Library of Congress Cataloging-in-Publication Data is available upon request.

ISBN 10:1-55783-700-7
ISBN 13:978-1-55783-700-4

www.applausepub.com

CONTENTS

INTRODUCTION

The monologue is an important tool of the actor. Well-performed, it reveals the actor's experience, intelligence, and potential. It is invaluable in the pursuit of a successful career in theatre.

As an actor you will undoubtedly need a monologue for a professional audition, an acting class, or a regional competition. What will guide your choice and how will you bring a single speech to a performance level? The task is formidable, but consider some of these suggestions as you work.

1. Choose a speech that moves you, one to which you personally respond. You might find it funny, painful, or even weird or upsetting, but somehow it pushes your buttons and you know that you can engage with it. In a class it's challenging to work on a character who differs from you substantially in age, ethnicity, or sexual orientation. However, in a professional situation you need to choose a character you'd be "right" for, for which you might be cast.

2. Next, read the entire play. Locate a copy of the full text in your library, or on the Internet, or read it in the bookstore, but read it. The character you have chosen may become an entirely different person during the course of the play, and your awareness of this can help you flesh out a performance.

3. Consider your audience. These selected monologues are directed at a variety of audiences. One twenty-first century trend is for

the character to speak directly to listeners. If your playwright indicates this, you must entertain a public speaking mode:

a. If the audience is large, make eye contact with someone in the first row, then move to house left and right and back, and even to the balcony, if there are people there. If the audience is composed of four or five auditioners, try to make eye contact with each;

b. Maintain a conversational tone, even though the house may be large. Decide what your objective is in speaking—are you explaining yourself, do you want the audience to like you, do you like it?

c. Keep gestures and movement to a minimum, and stay down center, or to one of the sides.

4. If you are speaking to someone on stage, locate the character. Is he or she sitting, standing? Close to you or at a distance? Does he or she move during your speech? Do you follow? Where are you? In a bedroom, kitchen, office, living room?

5. If your monologue is inward, a thoughtful reflection, consider where you are. Are you outdoors or indoors? (Compare Laurence Olivier's "To be or not to be" soliloquy while seated on a rock overlooking the ocean with Ethan Hawke's same monologue in the 2000 film production of *Hamlet*.)

6. Once you've made certain choices and worked on the delivery, you may have a keener sense of the character you want to bring to life. Then, how are you dressed? Do you have props to use (if appropriate)? A book, a glass, a telephone, a notebook—any specific object may be helpful.

After considering more than three hundred plays and admiring the spectrum of talent in the American theatre, we have chosen a variety of speeches that deal with the issues and conflicts that women of every age, ethnicity, and sexual orientation might face in our society. So you have many choices to make in the development of your performance, and extensive opportunities to be creative. Don't try to crash it together overnight; take your time and try it out a few times on friends. Take the challenge seriously and, as Stanislavsky said, "Love the art in yourself; not yourself in art."

NOTES ON THIS TEXT

In some scenes there are other characters onstage or characters who come on during the scene. To indicate this, we have included their speeches but bracketed them. Do not disregard them; your responses provide important clues for your character.

Some speeches might be longer than are called for in your situation. Again, the material may provide important clues to your motivation and background, but you may need to cut some in the interest of time. If so, mention to the audience that the speech is abridged.

ONE on ONE

THE BEST WOMEN'S MONOLOGUES

FOR THE 21ST CENTURY

ARE YOU READY?

BY DAVID AUBURN

While waiting for the chance to dine in a popular restaurant without a reservation, a WOMAN *jumps at the maitre d's offer for a table, but misses an opportunity for romance with the man ahead of her.*

SCENE
An upscale restaurant

TIME
The present

[(**MAITRE D'**: (*to* WOMAN.) Are you ready?)]

WOMAN: Yes! (*To us.*) Thank God. I was hungry. Also, I'm the food critic for the *Times,* and I've been anxious for some time now to get my claws into the throat of that *pompous evil weasel* of a restaurateur and rip him to absolute shreds for the benefit of my rather unusually loyal readership. I'm sorry. I'm not a vindictive person. I think I'm basically a decent person but I'd been watching people humiliating themselves for a table at that place for months, and the restaurant *sucks,* honestly: their foie gras is dry, their lapin en croute a l'Aubergine tastes like something my cat coughed up when it had the flu last winter, their wine list is emaciated, their syphilitic pastry chef couldn't frost a cupcake if you held a gun to his mother's head ... I'd been *dying* to get a crack at it but they wouldn't let me in, not even with a fake name. But tonight I was just walking by and I saw this nice-looking guy, just normal-looking, not a big celeb or anything—he was waiting for a table, so I thought, Why not me? Then I was offered a table and I *leaped* at it and now that supercilious creep is going to have a nasty surprise when he opens the paper tomorrow morning, I promise you. That does sound vindictive, doesn't it? I don't mean it to. I'm not a mean person. I'm just like anyone else. I like a decent meal. I like to rent a couple of videos and relax on a Sunday night. I like to drive up north for a weekend in the fall when the leaves start to turn. That sounds like a horrible personal ad, doesn't it? "Single Female, thirties, enjoys food, film, and foliage, seeks single male twenties-thirties for profound lifelong commitment" –Not that I'd ever *ever* write an ad like that—I'm not *desperate*, believe me, I'm *fine*. But all right, yes, I'd like to meet someone, I'd—I mean I *meet* plenty of people, At parties, or—Plenty of successful, brilliant, witty people—all right not plenty but some—and you try to be—but you know people get the paper, they read your stuff and you develop a reputation and even though you're just doing your job—like last month when I wrote that that new *unbelievably* expensive and pretentious sushi place downtown was enough to make an American feel a little less guilty about dropping the atomic bomb on Nagasaki—you can develop a reputation for, I don't know, harshness. And you start to wish you could make a clean break. You imagine what it would be like to meet someone totally *new*—like, I don't know, *anyone*—this guy here—just an attractive, well-dressed—I mean I'm not crazy about the tie, frankly, I would have gone with something a little less late-mid-eighties, but who cares? Doesn't matter. You have to be *flexible*. And you have to be ready: you couldn't plan it or hope for it. You would simply have to be prepared to recognize your chance when it came. When that person came along. I sometimes imagine something like that happening. Then I come to my senses and remind myself how unlikely that would be.

AT THE VANISHING POINT

BY NAOMI IIZUKA

RONNIE MARSTON, *a bacon packager at Fischers, a meatpacking plant, enters wearing a windbreaker, jeans, and work boots. She carries a six pack of beer in a plastic bag and lights a cigarette.*

SCENE
Story Avenue

TIME
The present.

RONNIE MARSTON: i got a cousin pete. i nearly ran him over the other day in my truck. i was on story avenue up where the road curves round real sharp, down by the greenway, where the pumping station's at, and you know how the cars, how they're always taking that turn a little too fast and some of em, they go skidding and they crash straight into that house that's right there with the brick that's all messed up from the cars that keep crashing into it, but that's all beside the point cause i wasn't speeding. i never speed. i'm a good driver, i never had a ticket in my life not a one, except for some dumb-ass parking tickets i never shoulda gotten in the first place, and then they had the nerve to tow my truck and that made me so mad, but i didn't have nothing to do with that little a-hole falling down, i did not push him, i did not lay a hand on him, but that's a whole other story i don't want to get into on account of a pending legal action. anyway this incident i'm talking about right now, this was all my cousin pete, it was all his fault. pete's got about ten lugnuts loose in his head, no common sense, none at all. my sisters, they're all so like, o poor pete. poor poor pete. and i'm like, to hell with pete. pete pisses me off. cause it ain't like he's slow. he ain't slow. he's just a screw-up is all. always getting himself into some kind of trouble cause he doesn't use his head, he doesn't think. pete volunteers now full time at the edison house over on washington. he's some kinda tour guide or something like that. he has this thing, see, he knows everything there is to know about thomas edison. you just ask him whatever you want to know, and he'll tell you. pete used to work at Fischers, but then he got let go on account of some situation I don't know the full details of. I work at fischers too. a lot of my family do — well two of my sisters and my brother-in-law, and his dad, and my dad, and my dad's brother, pete's dad, and peter's brother frank — anyway there i was, driving down story rounding that curve, and suddenly pete's right in front of me, he's just standing there all of a sudden running into the middle of the road, and thank god i got fast reflexes or i woulda run him over, so i slam on my brakes hard and i'm outta the truck in a flash, and i grab him and i'm up in his face shaking him and i'm like, what the hell is wrong with you i coulda run you over i coulda killed you just now. but pete he ain't even listening to me. he's babbling about seeing something down by the point, down by where beargrass creek lets out into the river, and did i know that the dead live on as particles of free-floating energy in the atmosphere like an electrical current or a sound wave and that's what ghosts are and do i wanna see what he's talking about, come see, ronnie, come and see. and i'm looking at him, and i'm thinking, this person, i'm related to this person. i'm related to him by blood and that just, that disturbs me. and i look at pete and he's still talking and finally i'm just like: pete. you know what pete. i really don't need this right now. i just got off work and it was one of those days. the feed tube broke, then the chlorine pump gave out, then the ammo line went tits up for three hours, and then if that weren't bad enough, the goddamn power goes out, some kinda short, who the hell knows. it's out all along mellwood and frankfort, all the way over to crescent hill. fifty-nine condemned hogs. we dumped near five thousand pounds of meat, and now my carpal tunnel is acting up and i don't even want to talk about the smell, you don't even want to know about the smell. so right now, pete, it's really not a good time for you to share with me your thoughts about the afterlife.

(*Pause.* RONNIE MARSTON *drinks her beer.*)

BAD DATES

BY THERESA REBECK

HALEY, *a successful restaurateur and single mom—in her late 30s, early 40s—thinks she's finally met Mr. Right. In the monologue she calls her brother for advice and then the no-show date.*

SCENE
HALEY*'s bedroom in a New York apartment*

TIME
The present

(SHE *looks at herself in the mirror for a long moment. Then, suddenly,* SHE *moves over to the bed, reaches for the phone and dials.*)

HALEY: Hey, it's me. No, not yet, he's coming over tonight. B.J. — stop it, I'm too nervous, you can't make fun of me right now. Yes. Ha ha. Yes, of course I got rid of her, she's spending the night at Emily's. No, honey, he more than assumes, it's been stated specifically, the plan is that he comes over, we order Chinese take-out and then actually do the deed on the living room floor before the food even gets here. (SHE *laughs.*) What? I guess. (SHE *checks her watch, moves, nervous.*) A little. (*Beat.*) A little, just a little, don't make it a big thing, it's a little. Okay, an hour, he's almost an hour late, but — oh don't do that silence thing. He's a busy guy, sometimes he's late. I'm not going to turn into one of those psycho girlfriends who thinks the worst when a guy's a little late. (*Beat.*) Shit. (*Beat.*) You think I should call him? It's just an hour. Of course I should call him. It's probably fine, right—yes I have his home number, I have his cell. I am not being stupid—B.J., stop it, would you—well, I will, I will call him. I will. Yes, I'll call you back of course I'll call you back.

(SHE *hangs up the phone.*)

(*Continuing; to herself.*) Jerk.

(SHE *paces now, nervous, picks up the phone, and starts to dial.*)

(*Continuing; on phone.*) Yeah, hi, Lewis? Uh, it's Haley, I was just wondering what happened to you. So, just give me a call when you get this, or maybe I'll see you first. You're probably on your way. Okay. Bye.

(SHE *hangs up, embarrassed at herself, puts the phone down. After a moment, SHE sits on the floor, putting her head between her legs, hyperventilating a little.*)

Shit. Shit.

(SHE *stands and moves around the room, nervous.*)

He's just late. People are late all the time. I am late all the time, all the time, that's so not true, I am never late, I'm too paranoid to be late.

(SHE *goes out into the hallway. After a moment, SHE returns with a phonebook, sets it on the bed and opens it.*)

Be here be here be here—yes.

(SHE *finds the number, shuts the book, and dials. Pause.*)

Oh. Hello! Hello, I was wondering, is, um, Lewis there? (*Beat.*) Uh, Haley.

(*There is a long beat.* SHE *looks up at the ceiling, trying to hold back tears, suddenly.*)

Yes, hello, Lewis. I uh, was wondering what happened to you, I think we said eight o'clock, and—Uh huh. Oh. Uh huh. (*Beat.*) Yeah, no of course, I'm not—angry, I'm disappointed, that's all. But not, I just, uh…. Listen, can I just ask, does that have anything to do with the woman who answered the phone? (*Beat.*) You did, yes, you told me about her but you said that had, that that had "gone south," and—

(*There is a pause.* HALEY *listens and nods her head.*)

Oh. Oh! You're living together. No, I, I'm sorry, I didn't understand that. I thought, "went south" meant, "went south." (*Quick beat.*) I'm not—accusing, oh Jesus, that's so—Listen, it's fine, I don't, I just thought something else was going on which obviously was my mistake. But I do, you know, I don't quite understand, why you didn't call. I mean, it sounds like you came to this decision sometime before this very instant. So my point being, were you even going to call and tell me about it? I mean, I've been waiting here for an hour and a half, expecting you to come over for some big romantic—and you clearly had no plans to come and were you just going to let me figure that out on my own in the most humiliating way possible? Okay, yeah, I guess I am angry, I—

(SHE *stops herself, trying not to lose it. After a moment,* SHE *takes a breath.*)

You know what? I don't want to talk about this anymore. I have to go. And don't come into my restaurant, even if someone as stupid as me calls you and invites you, don't even think about it, because you know what? We don't serve lying deceitful cheating fucking cowards.

THE BEGINNING OF AUGUST
BY TOM DONAGHY

JOYCE *is the recently widowed stepmother of a young man whose wife has left him.* SHE *cares for his new baby while he is at work. After drinking beer and tequila with the man hired to paint the house,* SHE *calls on an old friend.*

SCENE
The front lawn of a suburban house

TIME
The present

>(JOYCE, *in an apron and rubber gloves for cleaning, has just placed a call. After a moment, her caller picks up.*)

JOYCE: Hello, is this Cynthia Faunstauver? Cynthia, it's Joyce Tancreedi! Yes, it's Joyce Tancreedi. I can't believe I caught you in! Because I can't believe I caught you in, when you call people no one's ever home anymore! I know! Are you still with the softball at the middle school? Oooo, lacrosse. Well, I'm staying right near you! Yes, 203 Wild Arbor Lane. Yes, 203 Wild Arbor Lane! Well, it's a hop, skip and a fucking jump. I know, I'm sorry—I'm hanging out with young people and I'm cursing all the time now. Yes, I've been saying "shit" too! Now, look, Cynthia, short notice I know, mea culpa, I'm beating myself you can't see, but I'm having a few people over tomorrow. Give a person some warning, right? Well, whoever I can round up of the old group. The before-I-was-married group. (SHE *listens.*) Then you've heard. No, it's just so many people read the obit, so few called. Well, I just thought we could visit. And meet Jackie—Jackie is Jack's boy. It might reflect well on me, my friendship with you, in his eyes. Well, whenever is good, I'm just sitting here all day with the baby. Oh my gosh, yes, we've had a baby! That's why I'm even at 203 Wild Arbor Lane—this is where the baby is! Who is an angel, looking so much like Jackie, even this early. Her eyes with their questions. Even like my husband's—those two men I know, their eyes, just like them—though she's a girl and I've got that on my side! Don't I, Cynthia? I said she's a girl and—Yes, there's everything to catch up on! Jackie says it's an extraordinary time—and it is, Cynthia. So much! I'll call you in the morning then, Ta! (SHE *hangs up.*)

BOYS AND GIRLS

BY TOM DONAGHY

After agreeing to let REED, *her partner's best friend, move in to help raise their adopted son,* SHELLY, *a somewhat controlling, overworked, but highly successful professional, remains threatened by* REED *and* BEV*'s relationship. As tensions rise in this triangle,* SHELLY *throws* REED *out and* BEV *must choose between the two.* SHELLY *phones her mother, ostensibly to talk about the trip* SHE *is giving to her parents, but breaks down about losing* BEV.

SCENE
SHELLY*'s office*

TIME
The present

SHELLY: Hi, Mom, it's me. I wanted to go over the plans for your trip. I have the itinerary here. Because I paid for the tickets. I can send you a copy. It's just how they do it. It's just how it's done and there won't be confusion at the airport, no. I'll send you everything in advance. You'll have it *on your person*. So you're flying into Rome. No, it's just outside the city, it's — mmm — (SHE *looks*.) — it's called da Vinci, it's near the beach and then you — no, you're staying in the city in Trastevere. If Daddy wants to bring his bathing suit, fine, but Rome doesn't have a beach and the hotel doesn't have a pool. Should I be relaying all this to him, instead? Fine. You're welcome. You're welcome. You don't have to keep thanking me. Really, Mom stop or we'll have to talk later. You sent me that jelly as a thank you and I don't have time for all this gratitude. And I think—you know what I think? Forget it. No—you know what I think? It's some fucked up way of making me feel guilty somehow for being able to treat you and Dad so well. Just accept it and be grateful, tell your friends and don't keep feeling the need to express this forced gratitude.

(SHE *listens.*) She's fine. He's fine, he has the sniffles. Well, it's his birthday soon and then you can come over. No, he's on a business trip in Vancouver. He's been overextending a bit lately and he's gone a lot and—no. We've hired someone. A nice guy who has training. He's Swiss so he keeps everything running. I know you like Reed, everyone likes Reed, but we need this professional who's more consistent. That is what is important for a child. (SHE *listens.*) Good, so everything's working out and you fly to Rome and from there a bus to Umbria. Which is beautiful. It's where Bev and I—when we first met and couldn't afford Tuscany. I was still downtown and Bev was waitressing and we thought, OK, so not Tuscany, but someday! And then Umbria. So beautiful. How could Tuscany be better? And we thought maybe we found a, uh, new place. A new way. To do things. Based on disappointment. Which sets you off to someplace … unimagined … and—and—and she's left me, Mom. She took Georgie. We were at the beach. I don't know what I've done. I yelled at Reed, but I don't—I don't think that's it. It's been … I don't know what to do—we haven't been sleeping together and—what do I do? Mom? Mommy?

(SHE *listens.*) Uhuh. Uhuh. Uhuh. OK. No. OK. OK, sure. Then—have a good trip. No, we don't need to talk before you go. I'll have Sonia send you all the info. She's my new assistant. She puts up with me, but I think it's 'cause I pay her. I just wanted everything you had with Daddy. That's all. OK. Send him my love. And—and—to you too.

(SHE *hangs up the phone, puts some papers in a leather satchel, and makes a call to the outer office.*) Sonia? I'll be taking work home. I'd just rather be there today. Thank you. And Sonia? I just want to say you've been working out very well. Thank you for that.

BOXING IT

BY CHRISTINE EMMERT

A very large young woman stands before a tiny clear box. SHE is a street entertainer. SHE surveys the invisible crowd passing her by for a long minute.

SCENE
The Circular Quay at Sydney Harbor

TIME
The present

WOMAN: That's all right. Go about your business, it's a beautiful morning for it. For missing what is just under your nose. Yes, sir, that's right. It's me. Just under your nose. Keep walking. Keep moving. Don't stop to see something you won't see again in a blue moon. (SHE *stands still a long minute.*) Come on, all you need is ten minutes of my time. You can spare ten minutes, eh? What's ahead of you? A bloody day where you are tyrannized by a bloody boss. That's all. And then, the Pub. Drinks all round. Home to the telly. I might be the most exciting thing you encounter all week, all month. (SHE *gives up. Tries another side.*) Do you want to see something truly astounding? Not something like in the movies … but real. Here. In the sunlight. Just me and a box. What do you imagine we could do together? (*Smiles.*) Oh, you are a curious one. In fact, you're a naughty one. I like you. It's people like you change the world. (*Looks around and runs to other edge of stage.*) Yes, yes. I like a good crowd. Stay ten minutes. You won't be disappointed. I'm going to do something that will not even make you sorry you parted with money. Oh, don't hold on to your wallet. I'm just warming up the crowd. Gathering the crowd. (*Looks around happily.*) Yes, some more of you arrived. See me? See the box? That's the whole act. The whole routine. The box is there. I am here.

We need to get together, this box and I. We need to become one. How very Zen! Yes, I will fit myself into that little box. Great big me. Condensed. You laugh! I can see the smiles. You doubt that I can do it. I know you've heard of one born every minute. (*Listens.*) No, mate, I meant me. I meant I'm the one born every…oh, forget it! Got a chip on your shoulder, that's what you've got. Got out of bed on the wrong side…or alone. (*Laughs.*) That's what we like. To hear the laughter. In the morning. On the Circular Quay. So…(*Pauses a minute.*) Before I start trying to get this massive flesh in that little container, got to do some warm-ups. You don't think I could do this unless I got my muscles going, do you? Meanwhile I'll put a hat here for some preliminary palm-greasing. (*Puts the hat down and waits.*) Oh shy are we? How shy? I take all kinds of dollars. Yankee, Canadian, Aussie. I take Pounds, I take Euros. Rubles. Zlotys. Don't stop me now. I am a global taker! (*Looks to hat.*) Thanks. Ta. Let's get the pot started here. Just some encouragement for a poor starving sheila. (*Listens.*) What do you mean I don't look like I'm starving? Are you implying I'm well-nourished? Much nourished? I like to eat. That's why I've developed my talent. To earn my daily bread … Looks can be deceiving. I can be deceiving. I mean, the whole bloody point is that to look at me you'd never think I could fit in there. (*Points to the box.*) It took a lot of work. A lot of training to get this old body in that little space. A physicist would say it couldn't be done. (*Angrily.*) Oh, and are you a physicist? Oh you are. Well, you can pay up when I show you. But first, my warm-ups. (SHE *puts on music from a boombox and goes through a series of useless contortions.*) Fine, fine. Have your laugh. I'd like to see you fit in there. (*Points to box.*) I used to have a boyfriend that couldn't fit into a thing, if you get my meaning. Well, no need to get huffy. I didn't mean you. You're a bit past it to be my boyfriend. Now it will just take a minute. (*Looks in hat.*) Oh, I see we're being generous this morning. Two of us anyway. (*Sighs.*) Well, can't wait all day. Let me first say … (SHE *starts to put a toe into box.*) Just testing the waters. (*Stands in box.*) Oh, it's almost comfy. Well, it will be. Let me tell you that it wasn't easy at first. How did I get the idea?

(*Jumps out of box.*) I have to admit I was a little thinner then. Easier. I started learning this trick in India where my boyfriend lived. No, that's the boyfriend who didn't fit. This boyfriend used to tell me if I learned to put myself into a box I would have the discipline to see God. That's right! God! And since I'd never seen God, I thought—well now, let's give it a go.

The thing about the box is that you can't look at it as your enemy. You have to think of it as—well, a dancing partner. It's Fred and I'm Ginger. The music has begun … (*Changes music in boombox to something like a dance of old.*) You look at your partner. He takes your hand and … (*The lights change.*) It's rhythm, it's harmony … well, in actual fact, it's life at its finest. (SHE *starts to shrink and twist. At no time does* SHE *ever touch the box.*) Like all good efforts, it needs audience for appreciation. Don't go away or the illusion will evaporate. And wait with the questions! I'm in the process of transforming my molecules … into … (*Shrinks lower and lower until* SHE *is as compressed as* SHE *can be.*) There! Moving those atoms around. Shrink-wrapped. Shrinking. (*Mutters.*) I need a shrink. (*In a little voice.*) My kingdom for a shrink! (*Lights flashing.*) All right. Take your pictures. Show it around. Drop some money for me. There now. It's done. (*Lights come up.*) Done, I say. (*Looks in hat.*)

Oh, loverly, luv. That should get me some shrimp on the barbie. What's this? A condom? Hey, mate. I don't need a... Never mind. It's a beautiful day at Sidney Harbor. I can take a little fun. A little protection. Tell your friends. They'll never believe it. (*To someone who comes up to her.*) How did I do it? Mind over matter, of course. (*Counts the money, sitting on the box after turning it over.*) Christ, I got to get me a real job. This one needs some thinking... thinking outside the box. (Laughs.) Yeah. That's what it is. Outside the box. Inside the box. Boxing it. (SHE *takes her boombox, her box and her hat and goes off whistling.*)

BUNNY'S LAST NIGHT IN LIMBO
BY PETER PETRALIA

SISTER, *barely pubescent, hungry for affection, and in the midst of discovering the pleasures of masturbation, is obsessed with beauty products.* SHE *reverently spells the word of her favorite cosmetic.*

SCENE
The house SISTER *has been finished cleaning up.*

TIME
The present

SISTER: I love l-i-p-s-t-i-c-k. All kinds. I've got ten shades of red and five browns. "I have a color to match my every mood." I got that from a Revlon commercial. Do you know the one I mean? It's with Lynda Carter. You know, Wonder Woman? She's in the swimming pool? Never mind. I can't imagine the world without lipstick... it'd be pretty boring. I'd lose my favorite snack treat. (SHE *puts lipstick on and then bites a chunk of it. Then* SHE *puts it in her pocket as* SHE *chews the bite* SHE *took.*)

L-i-p-s-t-i-c-k is the world's most overlooked source for nutrition. It's packed full of healthy stuff like vitamins and oils. It goes on smooth and digests right away. Mmmmm. Mary Margaret says l-i-p-s-t-i-c-k is made out of bat poop, but I don't believe her. She doesn't know anything about beauty anyway. Her mom won't even let her wear l-i-p-s-t-i-c-k. My mother thinks beauty is important. That's why she is so pretty. She lets me wear makeup because she wants me to be pretty too. I'm glad 'cause being pretty is fun ... and important. I'm good at it, aren't I? I get all the boys to look at me. "My lipstick makes me look ... kissable." That's Maybelline. The boys in Mrs. Harper's class can't stop staring when I come in. I don't blame them. The other day on the playground I kissed a boy. He wasn't that good at it. I had to hold him down. He was chicken. He said he never kissed a girl before so I asked if he had ever kissed a boy and then he bit my lip. I got really mad so I told everyone that he liked boys. He's dumb anyway. Everyone made fun of him. He's a fag, I'm sure. (SHE *takes out the lipstick again to take another bite. But it's empty—no more lipstick in the tube.* SHE *sticks her tongue in the tube, trying to lick out every last bit.*) Hmmpf. I'm gonna have to get some more. I think I want "Tragic Diva" this time, from Urban Decay. It tastes better than Maybelline. I think it's because it costs more. They put special things in it that make it good ... and it stays on longer. I hope it's not bat poop. That Mary Margaret is crazy. They wouldn't put bat poop in there.

THE COMMITTEE
BY BRIAN DYKSTRA

CAITLIN *has come home to find her roommates engaged in a stupid argument about what color to paint a bench they left outside on the porch. After finding out her commissioned sculpture is to be cut in half,* SHE *decries the sorry state of affairs that allows her corporate benefactors to dictate actual artistic choices.*

SCENE
CAITLIN*'s apartment*

TIME
The present

CAITLIN: The arts committee. Their fucking arts committee happened. This corporate, racist, slimeball organization has an arts committee. An internal arts committee headed by MBAs who maybe took a couple drawing classes and thought they wanted to minor in art history or appreciation in undergraduate school at some second-rate state university in Southern California. It's made up of entry-level corporate lawyers who think the more committees they volunteer for, the better chance they'll have of surviving into the third year of their contract, when the real money kicks in. And they warned me. They did warn me about this arts committee. They said it had to get through that part of the process, but not to worry, it's really just a rubber stamp, just maybe a few fine-tuning suggestions, just a bit of polish maybe, but nothing major.

They want me to cut my fucking sculpture in half! They want the original design of the two intertwined bodies to be two separate sculptures that *suggest* the bodies are intertwined but are separated by about four feet because ... no, not to suggest some separateness that we are unable to close in our singular, computer chat-room, lap-dancing, cyber-sexual emptiness. But because they want one sculpture on this side, and one sculpture on this side, in order to frame the bottom entrance of their executive escalator. What the fuck is an executive escalator? Oh, and they want the woman's breast covered, not by any part of his body, but could she rotate away so that her right tit is hidden, except to the perverts who choose to make a special, circular trek around the sculpture, in order to ogle her stony boob. Probably through a leafy philodendron they're planning on snuggling up against it. Oh, and they want it multi-racial. This mother-fucking, racist organization, who just got embarrassed in the news a few months ago with leaked internal memos exposing its blatant racist and sexist promotional practices, wants to help cleanse its tarnished image by introducing separated, yet somehow still intertwined multi-racial figures. I'm using crystallized marble. That's some of the hardest shit there is to work with. You have to use a fucking diamond chisel. What do they think, I could just dye the shit? They want a brown face on one of the bodies. They said I could carve out an ebony mask and hands and feet and fasten it to the sculpture, or better yet, could I make it look like the dark face was *emerging* from the rest of the *statue.* Do you know how expensive crystallized marble is? And they want me to cover it with—Okay, to hell with it. I have to stop. If I keep talking about this, my head is going to explode and splatter brain fluid, skull bone, and gray matter all over this bench. Moratorium. No soothing, feel-sorry comfort, I'll just kill us all if I have to put up with that.

COMMUNICATING
THROUGH THE SUNSET
BY KERRI KOCHANSKI

The ethereal dusk serves as a backdrop for this drama about a pair of luckless teenagers confronting a violent past. RACHEL *is 16, pretty, and almost always distracted. There is something dark and sad lurking beneath her surface. Her friend* FRANKIE *has just said that* HE *loved tadpoles so much,* HE *ate them.*

SCENE
On a dirt hill in the Midwest at sunset

TIME
The present

RACHEL: Well, it's not like I went and fried up some tadpoles, Frankie. I mean, I *killed* somebody. Not just somebody. My *step*-brother—

(SHE *looks at him. Is uncomfortable.* HE *urges her to continue.*)

It's the way Jimmy looks at me when I say I'm sorry…And my mom… "Things like this happen to girls…Things like this happen to girls all the time…"

(*Seeing* HE *is listening,* SHE *begins to feel safe. Then suddenly,* SHE *lets it rip.*)

It just wasn't gonna be like those other times...Not when I was innocent and stupid—and seven years old—and didn't know enough until I read my books and realized—what Billy's doing to me...? It really is this horrible thing I think—Even though he says—

(SHE *stops. Begins to get upset. Calms a little.*)

See, when Dad died...

(SHE *stops. Begins to feel guilty.*)

He gave us food! Clothes! A place to live!—Jimmy...! He'd kick us out...

(*Beat.*)

And it would be back to the library...Or the woods...

(SHE *begins to explain.*)

And it wasn't all bad, Frankie. Not all the time...

(SHE *remembers, uncomfortable.*)

But some times...Like last...

(SHE *grows angry. Suddenly crying out, yelling.*)

Where is that man on the other side of the sunset...!? I want to ask him—If his step-brother was raping *him*—If he was so fat he couldn't even feel it, until he finally rolled off—'cause I was crazy—screaming at the world—crying at the sky—praying to Heaven...Wishing for some angel to fly down—Fly down to explain to me this thing I'd done—

(*Mystified.*)

Where'd the knife come from…? What had I done…?

(She *doesn't know what to do.*)

If no one would help—

(She *stands there, frozen.* He *moves to her, gently.*)

[**Frankie:** *You* helped, Rachel … You helped yourself…]

(They *stand. As* They *continue to stand,* She *calms. After a while,* She *moves away. Regaining her sanity,* She *moves over to the hill. Sits.* He *walks over. Sits beside her.* She *looks up at the sky.* He *looks up at the sky, too.* They *are in a different place now. After a while–*)

Rachel: The sun goes down over this hill, same as it does everywhere else…

THE DANCE
BY LENNING A. DAVIS JR.

SARAH *has spent a spinster's life with her sister* MILDRED, *her mother, and her sister's child,* GLEN. *Now in a rest home,* SHE *remembers, in a flashback, the time* MILDRED *revealed that* SHE *and* GLEN *were moving to Richmond, Virginia.* SHE *is devastated by the prospect of losing the nephew she loves so much.* MILDRED *has just entered the dance hall.*

SCENE
The Community Dance Hall in the Shenandoah Valley (in reality, the community room in a rest home)

TIME
1935 and 1948

SARAH: Poor little Glen. I wonder if I ought to tell him? If it came from me, maybe ... No! It isn't any of your business. He isn't yours ... But he loves his Sari. If he's awake, I just might give him the Babe Ruth. I hid in the spring house for his Saturday surprise ... You'd best get home to Mama. Why is it always me has to look after Mama? After all, Laurel is the oldest and she ... What made me say a crazy thing like that? I just forgot is all. Laurel's been gone almost 15 years now. But I mustn't let myself forget things. I must remember ... (*Pause.*)

(SARAH *is now 44.* SHE *musses her hair and closes her eyes.*)

Must remember! Must remember!... (*Opens her eyes and looks around.*) Is this supposed to be a treat? Some treat! Watching a bunch of crazies trying to dance....

Still, it's better than being in my room....I don't like sitting here like some kind of fool—everybody staring at me. I want to go back to my room. Where's Nurse Carter? I want to leave!—No, wait! There's something you must remember. Something...No, there isn't! Call Nurse...There is something! Wait! (*Thinks a moment, trying to remember. The effort is almost physically painful.*) Mildred! Yes, Mildred is coming to see me. (SHE *fusses with her hair and dress.*) Must look nice and neat so she'll take me out of this terrible place. She promised me as soon as I was well.

DEAD CITY

BY SHEILA CALLAGHAN

SAMANTHA, *40s, walks into a seedy basement bar exhausted, after a very emotionally trying day.*

SCENE
West 14th Street in New York City

TIME
The present

SAMANTHA: A vodka tonic, please. No, no. A water—Pellegrino? Great. I'm too nervous to drink... (SAMANTHA *notices someone in front of her.*) You look so familiar.... I knew it! I freelance there sometimes... oh, I'm sorry to hear that. Gosh, EVERYONE is getting laid off these days... what's wrong with your eye?... Oh. Is it contagious?... Oh.

(SAMANTHA *is served her drink.*)

Thanks. I've been having trouble finding work as well... no actually, my husband does. He sings at the—yes. Well thank you. I'm sure he'd appreciate that. Yes, he does very well these days. But you know, money isn't everything...

No no, I'm sticking with water for now …

(SAMANTHA *looks around.*)

It's so dark in here … no, I'd rather not drink, I have an appointment in a few hours and I'd like to be … well it was the closest place, or I would have gone to a coffee shop or some other … Home? No, I can't go home. It's complicated. What, what is happening to your eye?

(*Long, long pause.*)

How did you know that?

(*Even longer pause.*)

Baudrillard. 8 PM. The Hudson. We have an understanding.

(*A beat.*)

Yes, his booking agent … no, no I'm fine with everything, she's there right now actually, which is why I'm here…. Well he's good to me, you know, and I have THINGS we can afford THINGS … but I suppose the things I want most are, are not, you know I don't even know what they ARE? Ha. But … I'M A GOOD MOTHER … yes, my daughter is a Barbie doll but I, I don't, uh, I'M A GOOD WIFE … well my husband is a kite! And … My friends, okay, my friends are made of, of GAUZE, and … and sometimes I am not even here in this body. I'm a haze floating above it which is fine because it keeps me from THINKING and NO ONE KNOWS ANYTHING ABOUT ME!

(*A beat.* SHE *is embarrassed.*)

Ha, that, excuse me, I didn't … whew. It's been a, this day …

I passed the grave of a little boy this morning, still fresh, had a, a heart made of little blue flowers, and you know what? I, I bent over and … I ate the flowers…. One by one. Tearing flowers with your teeth, it's bitter, the juice is bitter and, and then your tongue goes numb. Isn't that just … I, I don't know the word, but you know? And I dream my son alive? Every night? He is twenty-two. He is long and lusty and tortured and has a tattoo of a, a raven on his belly, a black raven, and it HURT him when he got it, hurt so much he bit the inside of his cheek, and he welcomed the pain because it made him feel alive … I AM GETTING A TATTOO … I am a sensible woman, I AM GETTING A TATTOO BECAUSE I CAN'T REMEMBER HOW TO FEEL …

(*A beat.*)

You know we BOTH dream of our boy at night.

But. But they're different dreams. And some night we'll hold each other so tight that our dreams start to, to meld. And then we will have. One Small Thing. But. But we don't go to bed at the same time. So.

(SAMANTHA *drinks her Pellegrino, shaking.*)

Anyway. The economy will pick up. You'll find a job. Good to, to see you …

(SAMANTHA *puts money on the bar and exits quickly.*)

THE DIANALOGUES
BY LAUREL HAINES

This is a series of eleven monologues inspired by the public's continued obsession with the late Princess Diana, particularly among women. In "New York," a cab driver, CANDY, believes that her passenger is none other than Princess Diana, and offers some marital advice.

SCENE
Streets of New York

TIME
Sometime before August 1997

(*A New York cab.* CANDY, *the driver, picks up a passenger.*)

CANDY: Where to? Around? Lady, I don't just drive around, I ain't a sightseeing tour, you know what I'm saying? This is a cab. I go from here to there, I don't just... (*Turns back to audience holding a wad of bills.*) OK, you got it. I'll drive you around.

(*Drives.*)

You from out of town or something? (*Pause.*) OK, not the talkative type. You know, you really don't need to wear those sunglasses, my windows are tinted. Only people I know who wear sunglasses indoors are movie stars and my Uncle Rick. He got an eye shot out. Hey, wait a minute, you are a movie star! I know I've seen you before. Wait, wait, don't tell me. Melanie Griffith! No? OK, give me another chance. You're not a porn star, are you? Holy shit! I know who you are! You're Princess Diana! Holy shit! I've got Princess Diana in my cab! (She *turns fully around in her excitement.*) What the hell are you doing here? Huh? (She *faces forward and jerks the wheel.*) Hey! Watch where you're going! Oh my God. OK, OK, I'm cool. Princess Diana! (*Listens.*) Yeah, sure you're not. I know Princess Diana when I see her, and you're her. OK, fine, you want to pretend like you're not who you are, that's cool. I can do that. I won't say another word.

(*Silence.*)

So, like, what, you just wanna get out of the castle for a while, see a few sights? Figured you'd come to New York for some action? (*Pointing.*) Bet you don't see freaks like that at Buckingham Palace, do ya? OK, OK, I'll stop. I know what it's like for you royalty, always getting bugged by people. You probably just want some time alone. Hey, that's what's going on! You wanna get away from that husband of yours. Yeah, it's been all over the news. He's having an affair with that lady, whatsername, Camilla! Calling her on the phone and shit. Oh man, let me just say he must have his head up his ass. I mean, she is one ugly bitch! And you, you're beautiful, and glamorous. You're like, a princess! Hey, you're not thinking about getting back at him, are you? I mean, that's not why you're cruising around, is it? Because there are some real weirdos in New York; you should be careful who you pick up. Some guys look real nice, but they're psycho. The Wall Street types especially. It's always the clean-cut looking guys who turn out to have bodies in their refrigerators. I won't pick 'em up. And in this part of town, forget about it. Drug dealers and whores, that's all you got on this street. Hey, wait a minute, that's my cousin Denise! Denise!

(*Turning her head,* She *nearly runs into a truck and slams on the brakes.*)

Whoa! That was a close one. What were we talking about? Oh yeah, I mean, what guy gives up a princess for some butt-ugly broad? But you know something, it don't surprise me. I mean, men will (*Gestures.*), you know, anything that moves. You got to keep your eye on them. I got a lot of experience with that. My guy, James, when we first met he was like, oh Candy, I love you, you're so beautiful, you're my queen, right? And every day, he's going on about how gorgeous I am, and how I should be a model, and I'm like, yeah, you're beautiful too, James. And he's like, no baby, I got my face burned in a fire, I ain't beautiful, and I'm like, yeah, but James, you're beautiful inside. And he's like, no Candy, no, you, you're beautiful, you are, you, *you are beautiful.* And I'm like, OK, I'm beautiful. So we move in together, and we're in love, and we decide we're gonna get married as soon as I can get a divorce from my last husband. Well you can guess the rest of the story. One day, I come home from work, walk in the door, and he's on the floor with the deaf-mute girl from the dry cleaners. And she is a dog. I mean, worse than Parker-Bowles. This woman's face looks like scrambled eggs. And I'm so confused. Because I thought I was supposed to be so beautiful, and here he's been banging a circus freak. And he's like, oh baby, I'm sorry, I don't know what happened, please forgive me, and I'm like, oh no, no you don't. (*As James.*) But baby, baby, *I* can explain. (*As herself.*) Oh no, baby. I can explain. And I got my knife and — huh? Oh no, I didn't kill him. I just cut him up a little. Not a lot, just to scare him. That's what you gotta do with men, scare them. He don't fool around no more. (*Beat.*) That's what you gotta do with your husband. Just cut him a little. I bet he won't be expecting it from you. That's what'll make it twice as good. Dontcha think? Yeah, like one time when the two of you are eating your tea and crumpets and shit, and he gets up to make another phone call, you just go chk chk chk (*Makes a stabbing gesture.*) He won't be making no more phone calls after that, believe me!

(*Horn honks.*)

Oh go screw yourself!

(*To the passenger.*)

Huh? You wanna get out *here*? Oh no, you don't. This is not a good area of town. Believe me, you don't want to be walking around here at night, especially a gal like you. They'll eat you alive. No. I'm sorry. I can't let you out. I cannot be responsible for your certain rape and death. Or worse, one of these pimps might decide he likes you. "Princess Diana found turning tricks on Avenue C." No way. That's not gonna be on my shoulders. Well, yeah, by law I have to let you out wherever you want, but that don't mean I'm gonna. Yeah, you paid me. It's your ride. OK. OK, I'll let you out on one condition. You gotta take this. (She *holds out a knife.*) For protection. And whatever else you wanna use it for. Come on, take it. Yeah, there you go. (*To herself.*) Jesus.

(She *rolls down her window.*)

Hey, good luck, you know? I'm rooting for ya!

THE DIANALOGUES
BY LAUREL HAINES

In "Beaches," the pretentious STARLET *discusses the celebrity's right to privacy in the wake of Princess Diana's death, while simultaneously craving the attention of the paparazzi who court her.*

SCENE
Hollywood, or some version of it

TIME
Late 1990s

(*Cameras flash. A red carpet. A starlet in sunglasses stops to speak to the reporters.*)

STARLET: Thank you! Thank you all so much! I couldn't do it without you! (SHE *blows a kiss to the cameras.*)

My opinions? Why yes, I have many opinions on the subject. As you may know, I've been an advocate of privacy and stalking laws for quite awhile. I mean, celebrities have rights too. You might think that just because you see me on a magazine cover I'm not real. I am real! I have thoughts and feelings just like you. Feelings that get hurt when someone snaps a photograph of me and prints it under the caption, "Who's Getting Flabby"? And by the way, I gained that weight for a role. *The Life of Gertrude Stein*, my next film, opening Friday at a theater near you. And as you can see, I've lost every single ounce of it. So snap away!

(*The cameras go mad.*)

Oh yes, this new law had a tragic beginning. It's just terrible that Diana had to be killed in that car crash. But as my yogi says, out of tragedy comes tranquility. I think she would be happy to know that because of her death, others are able to live in peace. Why just the other day I was on the beach at my new vacation home in Malibu, and I realized my towel boy had a camera strapped to his thong. Thank God I saw it before I took my top off. I felt so violated! Well of course he said it was just for his mother, how many times have I heard that one? It's just such a comfort to know that because of this law, I can throw him in jail for six months instead of having my bodyguards hold his head under the surf. They're big men, but their arms get tired.

(*As if answering a question.*)

Well, I relate to her, I really do. It's awful to be wanted all the time. People just don't understand. I mean I can't go anywhere without people looking at me, following me, telling me how much they love me. When I became an actress, I never asked to be the center of attention! And I am an *actress*, I'm tired of you reporters identifying me as a "former adult-film star." I haven't done those movies for years. At least two years, and I've gone through the same training as Marilyn. All I want is respect. We celebrities work hard to get to the top. Do you have any idea what I did to get here? Well, of course you do, you've all rented the videos, but do you know what I went through *inside*? The pain, the suffering, the loss of innocence? Yes, innocence! Even I was once just a little girl in Kansas, growing up on my parents' farm, when one day they were killed in a horrible tractor crash and…wait a minute. Is that my story? No, that's my publicist's story. My story is…Where did I grow up? Oh right, New Jersey, but isn't that bad enough? New Jersey! The details aren't important. What matters is that I suffered. I was working at the mall! At Hot Dog on a Stick! And then when some man with a greasy mustache comes out of the blue and tells you he'll pay you $200 to…well, what was I to do? What would you do in that situation? No, don't answer that. You'd probably turn it down. You probably think you're better than me. And you'd be right. I'm just a cheap little whore! (She *starts to break down crying, then stops and looks up.*) A cheap little Oscar-nominated whore, so HA HA HA HA HA!

(She *gathers herself together.*)

Well, that's enough negativity. I'm going to release it now.

(She *does a yoga pose.*)

Aaaah. Well, they're calling me. I must be going. All right, just a few more photos.

(She *strikes a few poses while the cameras flash.*)

Oh you. The press. I love you, but I hate you. And I know you feel the same way about me. It's such a teasing relationship. You dig at me, I slap back at you, and then we all get in bed together and fuck like crazy! So I know you won't take this new law the wrong way. It doesn't mean I don't love you anymore. It just means you'll have to work a little harder to love me. But absence does make the heart grow fonder, and that's why I'm so glad I'll be able to take my next vacation to Malibu in peace. (*Beat.*) That's Malibu, on the South Shore. 1191 Coconut Lane. It's a private drive, but if you sneak through the service entrance no one will see you. (*Winks.*) I'll be waiting.

DOG ASSASSIN

BY STEPHEN A. SCHRUM

BOB *makes some extra money killing noisy dogs for bothered neighbors.* HE *then meets* AMBER, *who—typically, as* SHE *does with every man—falls in love with* HIM *after one encounter. In this monologue,* AMBER *calls* BOB *and leaves a phone message on his answering machine.*

SCENE
AMBER'*s apartment*

TIME
The morning after

AMBER: Hi, Bob! Uh, I never know what to say on these things. ... I hope you don't mind me calling you! Before I left this morning, I wrote your number down so I could call you and give you my number. It's really easy to remember: it's 555 followed by 4-3-2-1. It's like a countdown before a blast-off, one of my ex-boyfriends used to say. And he was really into phone sex! Oh! I guess I shouldn't talk about ex-boyfriends, should I? Ummmm. ... Well, that's my number: 555-4321. You won't forget it, will you? I hope not. I really want you to call me. Last night was very special to me. I never met anyone like you. I think you're really sensitive and sweet, and I want to see you again. I loved how you washed my hair in the shower this morning! Even my hairdresser isn't that gentle when he does it, and he's gay! Oh! I didn't mean to suggest you were gay, I just think you're really strong, and exciting, too! So call me, okay? I hope I'm not being too pushy, I know some guys don't like that, but I really want to see you again. (Pause.) Okay, I gotta go. Call me, please? You really made a difference in my life. Bye!

DOG MY CATS, OR THE STALKER PLAY

BY GAYLORD BREWER

Stinging from a recent divorce, a woman recounts her marriage's last harried days and a Valentine's Day "surprise" for her ex-husband.

SCENE
A city in America

TIME
The present

WOMAN: I told him, there's more to life than your exquisite bod, and anyway, abs as flat as a racetrack don't necessarily ensure a Formula One performance, if you take my meaning.

There he is, the he-man I married: male pattern baldness, chin stuck out like he's waiting for someone to slap him silly, a fat slob gone mad at the world who thinks he's Popeye the Sailor Man, toot toot. When I find the calorie counter in his briefcase, I can't even laugh. I tell him: Stud, we're a little late in the game for this nonsense, don't you think? You and me, we're strictly at the two-minute drill and it's time for a crass commercial break. He gets out the calculator and babbles about height-weight ratios, shows me a little blue notebook he's bought to track his progress. 1200 calories per day, he says. Desperate circumstances demand desperate actions, he tells me. He's been reading. Here's his entire menu: one half cans of carb-loaded, vitamin enhanced protein-busters; one half lite beer. Chewing a few carrots for roughage and to keep me excited. He moves his desk against the wall, sure enough, in come the new weights. Up go the charts and graphs, a photo of Brian Boitano. Don't ask me. I am being shown a side of this man I never asked to see.

The rest of the pathetic story: I can't even talk to my mom on the phone without the UH UH URGH *AAHH!* coming from the study. I say, hold on, mom—and listen, she's got her hands on a live one now, 29-year-old obstetrician, 20-freakin'-9, a blue-eyed baby with downy hair and love in his eyes and a *boat*; she's gonna eat him raw with a little salt and spit the bones, believe me—so I say, excuse me, Mom, that idiot's making love to his dumbbells and I can't even hear you. I go in, he's sitting there, curling with one hand, holding a pilsner in the other. I just stand in the door and don't say a word. He stops grunting, grabs a cigar in his manly paw and squints at me. I'm supposed to drop to the floor and raise my legs in a victory salute. I just stand there shaking my head. Then the beast speaks. He says, What are you staring at? I tell him, Go Eat Your Spinach, then I go back to Mom for the rest of the update.

So this Valentine's Day, why not?, I indulged in a little devil-may-care. Decked out in Frederick's finest: Red stretch vinyl top and mini, spike heel whip boots, "Bad Girl" cowboy hat, a little heart tattoo on my left thigh. Pure Sluts-R-Us.

Mailed a glossy over to muscleman's new bachelor pad. NO ENTRY, PAL! DO NOT PASS GO! Give him something to think about between reps. You want to see a TIGHT *BOD!?* Read it and weep.

That photographer was cute, too. Knew how to handle a lens. The beard, I'm not so sure about. He's calling back about negatives. Uh-huh.

DOTTIE

BY STACI SWEDEEN

A middle-aged woman with a Southern accent sits in a single chair. SHE *is wearing an orange prison jumpsuit.*

SCENE
A prison facility

TIME
The present

DOTTIE: Let me say—right at the top—that I'm essentially a good person. I know what you're thinking—that I'm self justifying, rationalizing, that anytime someone does something as "sneaky and low down, as two faced" as what I done, to quote the words of the DA, there *is* no essential goodness. That's where you'd be wrong. That's why I gotta lay it out for you in all the particulars. You'll see that I acted purely out of love, even if I am now forced to wear this here jump suit, unflattering in both style and color. Why didn't that ol' Martha Stewart get involved in something that could really make a difference in the life of inmates, like designing something a tad more attractive for daily wear?

Okay, enough of that. Here's what happened. My friend Chicklet— we call her that because she pops out kids like they was gum—has been going through a rough patch lately. Vernon left her. No big surprise there, he's always had a wandering, lazy eye. So Chicklet calls me, wailing and bawling like one of her own babies.

Dottie, she says, you gotta come over here and help me! I'm gonna go out of my mind! So, being the essentially good person that I am, I drop everything and rush right over. She lives across town, so it took me a while, what with all the new construction on 1-40 — and by the time I got there, great balls of fire! It was like a three ring circus, 'cept with no rings and in place of monkeys and elephants there is kids running wild.

No sooner do I walk in the door than Chicklet runs out. "Where you going?" I yell and she yells, "I'm gonna find that son of a bitch and kill him!" "What about the kids?" I yell. Chicklet just puts pedal to the metal and high tails it outta there.

Next thing I know a pair of grubby little hands has suckered onto me about thigh level. It's Melinda, wearing some kind of purple jelly all over her body and smelling to high heaven like a gigantic grape. Right behind her was Little Vernon, then Weldon, then the triplets — Cheryl, Carol and Meryl. I swear to god, they looked like some kinda refugees, with raggedy clothes, mismatched socks and hair sticking out in permanent bed head. It plum broke my heart.

Chicklet didn't want most of these kids and she ain't doing such a great job with most of them. And now, if she kills Vernon, these babies ain't gonna have no daddy. I almost started crying myself, thinking how all these kids was practically orphans in the offing.

That's when this gigantic light bulb went off in my head. Last Sunday at church after the *Show Yourself Friendly To Have Friends* sermon — Proverbs 18:24 — and before the coffee and cake, a couple women I know were bemoaning their infertility, saying that they were gonna leave it in the Lord's hand. Standing at Chicklet's it occurred to me that even the Lord might appreciate some extra help. I cleaned those kids up — and believe you me, Moses parting the Red Sea had it easy compared to my job. Then I loaded them in the car and dropped them all off on those ladies' doorsteps with a real nice note. "This kid needs *you*. Signed, the Lord's little helper."

So it was a real shock when Chicklet pressed charges. Then when that DA started calling me "sneaky and two faced" and saying that what I done was a class E felony of reckless endangerment, my feelings got real hurt. Now I'm serving three to seven. If that good Samaritan were alive today I'd say to him, brother, keep moving, cause they're gonna sue your scrawny ass. If something like this can happen to an essentially good person like me, good Lord. There ain't no telling what's in store for any of you. No telling at all.

ELEPHANT
BY MARGIE STOKLEY

At 17, MICHELLE *is bright and direct in her group therapy session.
Applying lipstick,* SHE *addresses the audience as the group.*

SCENE
The Soundview Institute, Tarrytown, New York

TIME
1998

MICHELLE: Hi. My name is Michelle (SHE *does a crazy gesture and noise
that somehow mocks suicide.*) Just kidding. No, really-thrilled to be
here. What do you want to know? What do you want me to say…

(*Silence.*)

Oh, wait, that's right. This is not a conversation—it's a session.
This is my time to share, with *complete strangers* how I feel … Well,
I feel like talking about trees. How do you feel about them? Wait.
Please, don't speak … let me. My fascination *stems* from this one
tree. (SHE *silently mouths "stems" again to emphasize the irony.*)
Rough crowd. (*A pause.*) Well, it's gigantic and right outside my
bedroom window. Some nights I feel like it wants in. Wants in
to my perfect pink-and-white-striped room. My room is perfect,

not because it's everything I want. It's just perfectly planned, the pillows, the balloon shades, the pictures, the bed, the window seat, my stuffed animals. I have even more animals under my bed. I have guilt about suffocating them … I feel … it doesn't matter. They don't match. (*A pause.*) They really don't. Well, it can't fall now because I just predicted it. What you think is going to happen — never does. It's a relief. You can't know it all. I just feel like in *my movie* that's what will happen. There'll be a huge thunderstorm with lightning, my tree will explode, and I'll be crushed. I can see myself split in half. I don't want to be surrounded by all those people who would need to be there if I got crushed. I am over groups. No offense.

ELEPHANT
BY MARGIE STOKLEY

A woman who has lost two sons in her lifetime, KATHLEEN *manages to present an upbeat façade. Here, using grandiose hand gestures,* SHE *describes the painful incident that precipitated her daughter's breakdown.*

SCENE
KATHLEEN*'s home in Montclair, New Jersey*

TIME
1998

KATHLEEN: "Nein! Nein! Nein!," we were screaming, but the puppy was having none of it. He was trained in German. I thought of every phrase possible to get him to stop—to no avail. He only bit Kyle once. Then his tail fell between his legs and he ran back into the garage. German shepherds are known for being able to anticipate. That's why they're working dogs. They herd sheep. Lead the blind. We should've given him a job, but now it's too late. The damage was done, but it could have been worse. His teeth are filed sharper than most knives. He was bred in Arizona, and all they have there is volcanic rock. He carries this one rock in his mouth wherever he goes. It wasn't his fault. Kyle is my nephew. He is only ten. He himself was an accident. My sister didn't mean to have another. Kyle is ten years younger than her eldest son. I am telling you this because he requires a lot of attention. I make up all these activities for him. Give him little rewards. Try to keep him active. I bet the sugar was to blame. It made him become raucous. It was the Fourth of July . . . our first family function since the funeral. All of us were trying to put on a happy face. (*Abrupt shift.*) When can I speak to Michelle? Well, I'd like to speak to my daughter. No, Mr. . . . I'm sorry, I forgot your name. Well, Tad, I know you are her counselor but I am her mother. I taught her how to speak and have been speaking with her every day . . . Fine. Explain your verbal deprivation method to me again! One more time. (*A pause.*) Tad, I have lost two sons . . . losing Michelle over the last few months is killing me. I am not trying to be difficult. I am trying to be a mother. (*A pause.*) Henry and I were distracted with cooking and entertaining our guests. It's hard to babysit when you're hosting. All the adults were gathered on the porch, and I guess Kyle, being out of our sight, took to jabbing Blaise with a stick through the gate. I believe Kyle liked hearing him bark. He talks. He makes these noises. (KATHLEEN *demonstrates* BLAISE's *howl.*) I don't know why Michelle opened the door and let Blaise out. My sister called the cops and the rest you know. The weeks that followed were miserable. As if life wasn't already rough enough, now my own daughter won't look me in the eye or talk to me in complete sentences. She shut down . . . I feared she would . . . she may have even tried. (*A pause.*) She was screaming "Nein," too. If that makes a difference. She let Blaise out, but she was devastated when she saw what was happening. We were all screaming, "Nein, Nein, Sitz, Nein, Sitz!"

THE EMPTY STAGE

BY MURRAY SCHISGAL

ALICE, *an actress in her 50s, is at a rehearsal.* SHE *is speaking to the audience.*

SCENE
Rehearsal auditorium

TIME
May 1990

ALICE: (*To audience.*) I have no objection to what we're doing. I agree wholeheartedly with Miss Pollack and I disagree wholeheartedly with Mr. Talevi.

(*Begrudgingly.*)

Leo. If our playwright and director are providing us with a forum to vent our genuine concerns … I unequivocally support them. It strikes me that theater nowadays is a bit of escapism that we cannot afford.

(*A beat.*)

Mrs. Alice Breen is my name. If I'm unfamiliar to you, the program will acquaint you with my credits. What I'm inordinately pleased about this evening is having a moment to speak to you as the state treasurer of ARF, that is an acronym for the Animal Rescue Fund. For those of you who haven't heard of our organization, let me begin by listing for you a number of dismaying statistics. This is not for the squeamish. For example, did you know that the McDonald restaurants boast of having sold sixty billion hamburgers? What they do not boast of is that in order to prepare those sixty billion hamburgers they have to destroy fifty million cows. Their famous clown spokesperson informs our children that hamburgers grow in hamburger patches and loooove to be eaten. Isn't that cute? He does not inform our children that hamburgers are ground up cows who have had their throats slit by knives or their brains bashed in by sledgehammers. So much for our famous clown.

(*A beat.*)

The average meat-eating American will devour during his lifetime one calf, three lambs, eleven cows, twenty-three hogs, forty-five turkeys, one thousand and ninety-seven chickens and fifteen thousand and six hundred and sixty-five eggs. Did you know that? And yet during the average meat-eating American's lifetime ... while enjoying hot dogs and hamburgers and veal cutlets, he or she will not confront the blatant reality that he or she is actually devouring pigs, cows and baby calves. Ninety-five percent of the animals we eat...

(SHE *breaks off, displeased.*)

Should any of my monologue be used, I'd be grateful if I'm permitted to complete mine before being interrupted by a phone call!

THE EMPTY STAGE

BY MURRAY SCHISGAL

A 20-year-old actress, Emma, *wanted to leave rehearsal early. It is now after three o'clock, and* She *is annoyed at not being released by* Ulee, *her director-father.*

SCENE
Rehearsal auditorium

TIME
1990

Emma: He had all this planned beforehand. My father has everything planned beforehand. Reality versus fiction. The death of tragedy. The impoverishment of imagination. Do you want to hear my father's favorite play? He says it was written by a friend of his who committed suicide. But I wouldn't take everything he says too seriously. Here it is. My father's favorite play.

(She *opens her mouth, miming Edvard Munch's "The Scream." The sound* She *keens is barely audible and no more than ten seconds.*)

That's it. The whole bag of potato chips. My father didn't cast me because I was so right for Lydia Simmons. I'm not. I'm too young. He cast me so I would ... reveal myself ... make public something that...

(*Sniffling.*)

…that's…private…between us. You'll have to forgive me if I start crying. Whenever I get into these situations…with him…I feel like such a baby…helpless…I'm ashamed of myself. In other situations, with other people, situations far more tense and…intimidating, I can take care of myself. I'm very good in emergencies. Ask anyone. But with him…

(SHE *hasn't cried;* SHE *takes a deep breath.*)

There…There's only two of us left. Maybe that has something to do with it. My mother passed away…several…years ago. Ovarian cancer. She was special and I…both of us…loved her…terribly…and we miss her…terribly. My father was a wonderful husband.

(*To* ULEE.)

Can I go home now? Did I do what you wanted?

(*Resigned now to tell all.*)

I was working in Garden Grove…in California…at the Gem Theatre…playing Mariana in Molière's *The Miser*.

I met a…young man there, Chance Wemple. He's not in the theater. He has a temporary job in a 7-11 store…as a grocery clerk…and…when my father came out to direct *Midsummer Night's Dream* at the Old Globe in San Diego…I introduced him to…Chance. I thought they'd get along. I thought my father would appreciate Chance's radical politics and commitment to the environment and…it was unforgivably dumb of me. I've never been so embarrassed in my life.

The way my father spoke to him … It was rude and … vile! Chance is thirty-four years old, fourteen years older than I am. He was wearing jeans, hiking boots, a flannel plaid shirt, a leather wristband and a silver earring. He has long blond hair, to his shoulders, which he doesn't comb, and he doesn't shave every day either, but he is very, very, very physically attractive. He plans to be a sports journalist. He's an avid sports enthusiast and an excellent writer.

What my father doesn't know is that Chance has connections with several newspapers in the Midwest. In the next few weeks he's being interviewed by editors for a job writing a column on local and national sports.

What you have to know about my father is that he's a bitter and disillusioned man. He was once a radical himself, very active politically. To show you how much … I was named Emma after Emma Goldman, the socialist anarchist who in the early part of the last century was our most courageous and outspoken advocate for individual freedom and minority rights. When my father went to college, he was a member of SDS, Students for a Democratic Society. And he was a leader in the student riots protesting the United States invasion of Cambodia during the Vietnam war. The college my father went to was Kent State University.

When other little girls were listening to their fathers reading "Goodnight Moon," I was listening to my father telling me the story of what took place on the Kent State campus during a four-day period in May of 1970. Do you want to test my memory, Daddy?

We used to hold a private memorial service in May for the four students who were killed by National Guard soldiers. We'd light a candle on the kitchen table and we'd be silent for a minute and then my father would spell out each letter of their names.

(SHE *clasps her hands; intones solemnly.*)

Sandra Lee Scheur, S C H E U R. Allison B. Krause. K R A U S E. Jeffrey Glenn Miller. M I L L E R. William K. Schroeder. S C H R O E D E R.

(SHE *turns to* ULEE.)

How's my memory? Not bad, huh?

(SHE *faces front.*)

Oh, incidentally, my father was one of the nine students wounded at Kent State. A bullet splintered a bone in his leg and he's been disabled ever since.

(*To* ULEE.)

I'm sorry I disappointed you. I'm sorry I didn't fulfill your dreams about me. I'm really sorry, okay?

Aren't you going to say anything?

(*A beat.*)

Daddy?

ENTER THE NIGHT

BY MARIA IRENE FORNES

PAULA, *whose life has been involved with her farm, tells her friend*
TRESSA *of her need to keep working, despite her serious illness.*

SCENE
PAULA'*s bedroom*

TIME
The present

PAULA: (*Lying on the bench.*) I'm not well. But I act as if I am. As if
I've been told by a doctor that I'm well, and I can go ahead and do
whatever I want. Well, I haven't been told that. If I stop taking my
heart pills, I'll die.

Yes. — I keep doing the work on the farm and I keep saying, "It's
not going to harm me." I keep saying that. But there's a voice inside
me that tells me, "If you keep doing what you're doing you're going
to die. The next shovel you push through the dirt will kill you."
(*As if replying to herself.*) "This is good for me." If I carry a sack of
feed:

"This has to be good for me." I can't just stand there and let
everything I've worked for go to waste, sit and let the animals lie

on their own manure, uncared for, let them starve and die. Let them get sick and die. I can't do that. I can't just let my meadows go to waste. I can't sit there and watch the weeds take over and do nothing. That's not the way I am. I'd rather die. I don't want to be different from the way I am. I don't want to be a different person just to stay alive. If the person I am dies, then I die. — If taking care of what I love kills me, then I want to die. — "It's a Russian roulette," the voice says. "Every time you climb a ladder or pick up a bag of feed or a bucket of manure it can be the last." (*Pause.*) I can die. (*Snapping her fingers.*) Just like that. — Next time you run after a sheep. (*Snaps her fingers.*) Like that! (*Standing.*) I can't afford to pay someone to take care of things. (*Showing* TRESSA *the palms of her hands.*) Look at my hands.

Pete wants to help. He has gotten in debt for me. But he can't borrow any more. He's lost his credit. He's done all he can to help … can't ask him to do any more. He humiliates himself for me. They won't lend him any more money. I can't bear it. You'd think I'd make enough money selling the milk and the wool and the eggs. But I don't. I don't know how to make it work. It costs more to feed the animals than what you could earn from them. I owe that money to Peter. I want to pay him back. He says not to be silly, that he's my husband and besides he is my partner. But that's not so. He's gone into it just to help me. He's never understood why I do it — keep my hands in the dirt all day long. I don't want to ask him for money and I still do it. I ask him for more money. It's a loan. I always say it's a loan. I've never looked kindly on people who can't take care of themselves and their obsessions or their vices; people who make excuses for themselves and make others pay their bill. That's what I'm doing. I know I should sell the animals and most of the land. But I can't. I'm like a drug addict who will do anything to satisfy her vice. I've lost my faith, my honor, my sense of pride. I still have them though … (*As if seeing them.*) I still have them … running in my meadow.

(PAULA *looks at her hands.*) I do the work because I have to. Because I can't afford to get help. If I don't I would have to watch them starve to death. Do you think I could sit there and watch them die in a swamp of manure? I couldn't. I would die before them. I couldn't stand seeing them suffer....Oh, Paula ... (*Standing and crossing to the right of the bench and sitting.*) Oh, Paula.—Don't worry. Don't worry. It doesn't matter. My life is over.—There's nothing to worry about.

FABULATION, OR THE RE-EDUCATION OF UNDINE

BY LYNN NOTTAGE

A successful African-American businesswoman until her husband absconded with all her money, UNDINE *is forced to return to her childhood home in the projects in Brooklyn, only to face an even more painful reality. Proud and ambitious,* SHE *tells her story with wit and self-awareness.*

SCENE
UNDINE*'s office in New York*

TIME
The present

UNDINE: (*To audience.*) This is where the story will begin. It is mid-thought, I know, but it is the beginning. In the next twenty seconds I will experience a pain in my chest so severe, that I've given it a short simple ugly name. Edna. Forgive me, I *am* Undine Barnes Calles. Yes. I left home at thirteen. I was a bright child. I won a competitive scholarship through a better chance program to an elite boarding school in New England. I subsequently acquired a taste for things my provincial Brooklyn upbringing could no longer provide. I went to Dartmouth College, met and mingled with people in a constructive way, built a list of friends that would prove valuable years down the line. And my family ... they tragically perished in a fire, at least that's what was reported in *Black Enterprise.* It was a misprint, but I nevertheless embraced it as the truth. Fourteen years ago, I opened my own very fierce boutique PR firm catering to the vanity and confusion of the African-American nouveau riche. And all seemed complete when I met my husband Hervé at a much too fabulous New Year's Eve Party at a client's penthouse....

[(HERVÉ *enters.* HE *wears a well-constructed suit, he moves with the grace of a flamenco dancer.* HE *holds a broccoli spear between his fingers.*)]

He was standing by the crudités dipping broccoli spears into the dip. He did it with such flair that I found myself hovering around the hors d'oeuvres table for most of the evening. I watched, dazzled, as he sucked the dill dip off the vegetable with his full lips.

[(HE *pops the broccoli spear into his mouth and wipes his lips with a napkin.*)]

Up until then I'd been dating a rapper at the twilight of his career. [(*Rapper Boyfriend enters.*)] He'd become addicted to pain-killers and his paranoia was making the relationship tiresome, he'd drive around Bushwick, Brooklyn, in his SUV, tunes pumping, yearning for ghetto authenticity. His six-figure income had isolated him from the folks. But nevertheless, he was becoming more ghetto by the moment. Too ghetto for the ghetto. [(*Hervé goes over to Undine; their eyes lock.*)] Hervé looked over at me, I was five, I was twelve, I was seventeen. I was twenty-eight. I explored the full range of my sexual awakening in that moment. As he approached I could not move my feet, and actually felt something I read a million times in romance novels, a tingle in my loins.

[HERVE (*With thick Argentine accent*): Hello.]

UNDINE: Hello. Did you enjoy the dip? (*To Audience.*) I could think of nothing cleverer to say and averted my gaze. Then I glanced at my boyfriend with the hostess and a Philly blunt between his fingers. And I channeled all the charm in the universe.

(*To Hervé.*) It is almost midnight and I see that you're alone.

THE FACE IN THE MIRROR

BY PHIL ZWERLING

BECCA *is an 18-year-old black confined in the Los Angeles Juvenile Hall awaiting trial on drug charges. Huffing glue in the bathroom with friend* LIL' SHIRLEY TILSON, BECCA *has just seen a frightening apparition in the mirror and runs into the recreation room to tell the other girls.*

SCENE
The women's rec room

TIME
October 31, 2004

(*A piercing scream is heard offstage.* BECCA *enters, breathless.*)

BECCA: She good. She was dead stoned. She never saw the witch.

I seen her, I'm the one scared to shit. I'm the one needs the shrink.

(SHE *slumps into the chair.*)

I saw her. I saw a old witch. A ugly old witch. Ugly. She was uglier than you ... and that's ugly. I seen death. I ain't scared of you or

Big Donna. I seen death in her eyes. I seen death. In the mirror. The cracked one in the shitter. She was there! Lookin' out at us. Lil' Shirley hit the bag first and I held her when she lay back. I could hear you all startin' to make noise in here but it was nice and peaceful where we was. Then I looked up. The mirror was cloudy. Like smoke, you know? At first I couldn't make anything out. Then this face … this ugly face … grew in the mirror. She was alive, I could see by her skin, and she was crying, but her eyes was dead … like a fish after you cut off the head.

(*A beat.*)

But, it wasn't no fish.

Her hair was long and messed up like she didn't have no comb and the wind had blew it all around and she didn't care. Her clothes was black. Black shirt, black dress, black robe. Black everything … and long, black fingernails, but her skin was white, really white. She didn't say nothing, but I knew she came because tomorrow's the Day of the Dead, and she's looking for her children. Her dead children. She came to take me … or Lil' Shirley … or both of us.

(*Thinking.*)

She was crying, though. Crying and sad … (*Beat.*) and dead.

FAT PIG

BY NEIL LABUTE

HELEN, *a very overweight woman, is in a relationship with* TOM, *who has brought her to a company party at the beach.* SHE *senses his reluctance to mingle with the others, and worries that he is embarrassed about her appearance.*

SCENE
A stretch of sand at the ocean

TIME
The present

HELEN: Tom, you are aware that I like you ... you already know that.

[TOM: Yes.]

HELEN: But I get the feeling ... I mean it is now pretty obvious that there are some problems here. Issues, or whatever. And we need to get over them or ... well, you know. Things that I don't wanna think about.

[TOM: I guess.]

HELEN: Please, you need to stay in this. Focused on it, so don't drift off or anything. I love you so much, I really do, Tom. Feel a connection with you that I haven't allowed myself to dream of, let alone be a part of, in so long. Maybe ever. But I can't be with you if you're feeling something other than that same thing that I am … completely and utterly open to that other person. I don't know what to say here, Tom … I'm worried sick. Look at me … when did you ever see me not eat a hot dog that was placed in front of me? Huh? (*Tries to chuckle.*) I know you hate those jokes, sorry, but I'm … Tom, tell me about it. I know you're thinking something, so we might as well just … one more thing. Just this. And I've never said this to anyone, not any other person in the world. Ever. My parents or a … no one. I would change for you. I would. I don't mean Slim Fast or that one diet that the guy on TV did … with the sandwiches from Subway. That guy…

[TOM: Helen … that … that's not…]

HELEN: I'll do something radical to myself if you want me to. Like be stapled or have some surgery or whatever it takes—one of those rings—because I do not want this to end. I'm willing to do that, because of what you mean to me. The kind of, just, *ecstasy* that you've brought me. So … I just wanted you to know that.

FEATHER
BY CLAUDIA BARNETT

Stalked by a dream demon who looks exactly like her husband, NATALIE *dedicates herself to painting her nightmare images, transforming herself into an artist, and her bedroom into a gallery. The Demon watches her as* SHE *rises from her bed, disheveled, and speaks.*

SCENE
A bedroom

TIME
The present

NATALIE: Ada and I decided to walk home from the party together. We had discovered earlier that we both lived on the same street, and neither of us had a car. Someone offered us a ride, someone who wanted to take Ada home, but she said no, we wanted the exercise and the air. I didn't mind; I did want the exercise and the air, and I was fascinated by this blond beauty's presence among my darker, louder friends.

The streets snaked in loops, and I hadn't lived there long, so I followed Ada without a thought, not realizing that she was following me.

We turned onto a long road leading down a steep hill. The left side was a stone wall. The right side was the edge of a cliff. I peered down at the tops of trees, a sea of dark green.

Ada grabbed my arm and said it wasn't safe, and I asked her if there was another way to walk. That was when we discovered we were lost.

She looked down the road and back at me with a glance that looked like hate but could have been the way the moon caught her eyes, and said we needed to hurry. We walked in silence until we heard a car motor behind us, and Ada tensed again. The car stopped, and before the door even opened, Ada yelled "Run!"

I looked back at the car and saw a man's silhouette emerge.

I ran behind Ada, thinking of my party shoes.

Then I heard another motor and looked back. A motorcycle had parked beside the car, and my first thought was that the car man needed help, and the motorcycle was the police, and I could run slower now.

But Ada yelled more urgently, and I followed.

Then I heard footsteps, two sets, and I looked back and saw the two men.

They were moving quickly but then stopped and bent down, and then they were holding something in their hands.

I ran.

Ada was far ahead, just a red spot down the road, a tiny fleck the color of her dress.

The road continued with no end in sight, all wall on the left and cliff on the right. I was looking for a place to hide.

I listened to my heels click against the pavement as I ran. I thought I might fall, and then I thought that thinking about falling might make me fall, and then I realized the men were approaching me quickly.

I turned around and one was less than 10 feet away. He was aiming a weapon at my head, possibly a rock.

I froze.

Then suddenly he tossed it toward me and I surprised us both by catching it. It was a tennis ball.

The men raced past me, leaving me in shock on the road.

It was Ada they were after, Ada they would catch.

I felt, all at once:

Helpless. I knew I couldn't reach them, and even if I did, there was nothing I could do.

Stupid. For having said no to the ride.

Guilty. Because it wasn't me.

Relieved. Because it wasn't me.

Jealous. Because it wasn't me.

I recognized the jealousy from junior high, a residual response from always being chosen last at gym, from never having been asked to the prom.

It was an inappropriate reaction. I realized that, even as I heard Ada scream. I found that I was running. I had been, ever since I'd caught the ball, and there were the two men ahead of me, standing in the street, looking over the edge of the cliff, where Ada had jumped into the trees.

The only other thing I can remember is looking down into the trees and seeing Ada's red dress in the sea of green.

FIT FOR FEET
BY JORDAN HARRISON

In her late 20s, CLAIRE *is about to marry* JIMMY, *although she is worried about his mental state.* HE *is obsessed with the great Russian dancer, Nijinsky; in fact,* HE *believes that he is Nijinsky.*

SCENE
CLAIRE *and her mother* LINDA *sitting in Adirondack chairs*

TIME
The present

CLAIRE: Last night he climbed out of bed, sleepwalking, he does that.

[(*Jimmy enters, his arms stretched out, somnambulist style.*)]

But never like this, all the way downstairs and out the front door. I put on a raincoat and followed him.

[LINDA: A raincoat! With all your beautiful things ...]

CLAIRE: The most worrisome thing was he didn't trip once. Used to be he couldn't walk for his own shoelaces. Here he was, a bounce in his step.

Sidestepping cracks, sashaying past puddles, softly snoring all the time.

Soon we're in a part of town I've never been to.

Cobblestones, steaming potholes. Can those be gaslights?

Can't even catch sight of a Starbucks.

He seems to be practicing steps.

His arms striking the air, his legs like scissors.

As I watch him, I can almost hear the music he's dancing to.

And it's like he's lighter on his feet with every step.

People notice. All the motleys out at 3 AM:

Insomniacs with dark rings, child molesters, women with frosted hair.

(*Linda gasps*)

They all come out of the shadows and follow him,

They don't know why. How can they not?

Soon it's a little parade of freaks, with Jimmy at the head like a drum major.

And then he takes off.

(*Stage right,* JIMMY *leaps into the air, hovers there, and lofts another inch before landing.* CLAIRE'*s hand at her mouth.*)

I'm peeking from behind a dumpster in my old raincoat.

My hair flat around my shoulders like a wet rat.

And I don't have anything to do with that brilliant thing in the air.

And he has even less to do with Jimmy.

Enough. I break the spell. I shake him awake

He feels small in my arms, all the people watching us.

Then his eyes open on me, ash-black, and he says, "You try to keep me…

[JIMMY: (*Overlapping*) You try to keep me down with the scalyskins and the black-eyed beasts but you are death. I am life and you are death.]

[LINDA: One should never wake people in the middle of dreams.]

CLAIRE: Tomorrow we walk down the aisle and I'm *death?*

A FRIDAY NIGHT TRANS-AM RIDE

BY ANDREA MOON

CAROLINE, *a young woman of the middle class, economically and morally speaking, is an artist and intellectual. On her first visit to the county jail to see her Vietnamese friend Trang,* SHE *fell apart and left abruptly. On this visit,* SHE *is trying to maintain control and communicate by telephone through the glass separating them.*

SCENE
CAROLINE *is sitting in Booth H of the jail's visiting room*

TIME
The present

(CAROLINE *glances around quickly, then reaches down into her pants, removes a wet wipe, and starts cleaning the phone.* SHE *looks up and smiles.* SHE *puts the phone to her ear and holds up the wet wipe.*)

CAROLINE: A friend gave it to me. So. Hi. It's much quieter this time of day. Though I was still in line for like an hour. I swear the porkos downstairs just pretend to be busy, just to keep you waiting. Some kind of power trip. The way it's all set up, it would make an interesting psychological study. Them in their own little plexiglass prisons, only elevated above you, of course. So they can look down their noses at you. I wouldn't think I'd be susceptible but I am. I threw up a couple of fifty-cent words when talking to the guard, trying to prove, I don't even know what.

Why are you letting me ramble on like this? None of this is what I want to say to you. I'm sorry about last time. I lost it. I'm not as strong as, as I'd like to be. Or as I've witnessed people being. It was too much, the incongruity of this … this … situation, you in this hole and reciting poetry to me. I. Angry. I wanted to be. I don't know. It could be worse. It could be worse for you. Listen, I remember when my mother died. And Susan called you. You drove twelve hundred miles and showed up on my doorstep at eleven o'clock at night. I was awake, sitting in that black leather rocker. I'd been awake and rocking for like two days. You came in with a bouquet of daisies that you'd obviously picked from the side of the road somewhere and by the look of them at least twelve hours previous, and you said, "Did somebody order flowers?" and I said, "If I see one more flower I'm going to puke," and you threw them over your shoulder and said, "Good, because there's not a single flower shop between here and Chicago." And you said, you said, "This will have to do," and you pulled out that Rumi book and you rubbed my feet, you rubbed my feet and read me Rumi for somewhere around twelve hours until I fell asleep. That was my first Rumi experience. I'm not torturing myself. It's the opposite. It's my Friday night Trans-Am ride. Nothing. A poem. You wouldn't know her. She's not famous. Angel. No last name, just Angel. I don't have it memorized. It's just something I'm holding onto. To keep me human. You? What are you holding onto? (SHE *listens.* SHE *smiles.* SHE *puts her hand up on the glass and holds it there*).

GEM OF THE OCEAN

BY AUGUST WILSON

AUNT ESTER, *a very old, yet vital, spiritual advisor to the community tells* MR. CITIZEN, *who has come to her for guidance, about her journey to America and where those who did not survive reside.*

SCENE
In the kitchen of Aunt Ester, Eli, and Black Mary

TIME
1904

AUNT ESTER: Black Mary, go get the map. I got something I want to show Mr. Citizen.

(BLACK MARY *exits up the stairs.*)

Some people don't like adventure, Mr. Citizen. They stay home. Like me. I done seen all the adventure I want to see. I been across the water. I seen both sides of it. I know about the water. The water has its secrets the way the land has it secrets. Some know about the land. Some know about the water. But there is some that know about the land and the water. They got both sides of it. Then you got the fire. That's a special one. It's got lots of secrets. Fire will heal and kill. It's tricky like that. I can talk about the land and I can talk about the fire. But I don't talk about the water. There was a time, Mr. Citizen, when God moved on the water. And sometime he moves on the land. Is he moving now? We don't know. We can't all the time see it.

(BLACK MARY *enters with a quilt on which there is a map.*)

Take a look at this map, Mr. Citizen. See that right there…that's a city. It's only a half mile by a half mile but that's a city. It's made of bones. Pearly white bones. All the buildings and everything is made of bones. I seen it. I been there, Mr. Citizen. My mother live there. I got an aunt and three uncles down there in that city made of bones. You want to go there, Mr. Citizen? I can take you there if you want to go. That's the center of the world. In time it will all come to light. The people made a kingdom out of nothing. They were the people that didn't make it across the water. They sat down right there. They say "Let's make a kingdom. Let's make a city of bones." The people got a burning tongue, Mr. Citizen. Their mouths are on fire with song. That water can't put it out. That song is powerful. It rise up and come across the water. Ten thousand tongues and ten thousand chariots coming across the water. They on their way, Mr. Citizen. They coming across the water. Ten thousand hands and feet coming across the water. They on their way. I came across that ocean, Mr. Citizen. I cried. I had lost everything. Everything I had ever known in this life I lost that. I cried a ocean of tears. Did you ever lose anything like that, Mr. Citizen? Where you so lost the only thing that can guide you is the stars. That's all I had left. Everything I had ever known was gone to me. The only thing I had was the stars. I say well I got something. I wanted to hold on to them so I started naming them. I named them after my children. I say there go Cephus and that's Jasper and that's Cecilia, and that big one over there that's Junebug. You ever look at the stars, Mr. Citizen? I bet you seen my Junebug and didn't even know it. You come by here sometime when the stars are out and I'll show you my Junebug. You come by anytime you want. You got the stars but it's that wind what drive the boat, Mr. Citizen. Without the wind it would just sit there. But who drives the wind? What god drives the wind? That's what I asked myself but I didn't have no answer. So I just started singing. Just singing quietly to myself some song my mother had taught me. After that it was all right for a little while. But the wind did drive the boat right across the water. What it was driving me to I didn't know. That's what made it so hard. And I didn't have my mother to tell me. That made it harder.

THE GHOST MOMENTS

BY RANDY WYATT

"The Ghost Moments" is an evening of stand-alone monologues bound together thematically. Issues of "hauntings" and "exorcisms" are explored. In "All Nighter," ELLIE, a young married woman, sits in a chair with a blanket around her.

SCENE
A comfortable living room or den

TIME
The present

ELLIE: Every so often, I stay up all night. You must think I'm crazy, I know my husband does. He keeps telling me that we're both way too old to do that crazy college kid stuff. I think it's just him trying to drag me down the path of getting older with him. I'm in denial, he says, and I tell him if being in denial means being scrupulously exact about your birthday candles, then baby, I'm in denial and I'm setting up shop.

He shakes his head and shuffles off to bed, and I stay up. I know he wonders what I do, but really, I don't do much. I flip the channels, I wash windows, I check and recheck the oven burners. I listen to my children snore. I listen to the wind howl outside and I think about shelter. I'll pour myself a glass of milk and realize "Here I am, pouring a glass of milk. I can do that. I am able to pour a glass of milk whenever I want to."

And I'll sit in the kitchen with my 3 AM glass of milk, and I will look around me, and look at all the stuff—the telephone, the car keys, the chair I'm sitting in. And realize it's all ours. Or I will stare at my hand for the longest time, moving each knuckle slowly, knowing that even this is a gift. And by 6, when my husband's alarm starts going off, it's like I have had a new baptism, a brand new perspective. It's the only time I ever don't mind being sleepy, when I can kiss my husband in the morning, giggle at his rolled eyes at me, send my adorable, healthy, chattering kids off to school, to let them take another step towards being themselves. And when the house is quiet again, I call the boss and let him know I'll be in later on Monday. Then I go upstairs, and I pull the comforter up around me, close to my face, and I am acutely aware of how wonderful sleep is, how wonderful my blankets are, how wonderful this kind of denial can be. How wonderful everything is. Wonderful, wonderful, wonderful.

(She *falls asleep.*)

THE GHOST MOMENTS

In "Water: A Memoir," an older woman, Caroline, *takes a sabbatical from her life in order to remember, to renew, and to celebrate it.*

SCENE
Niagara Falls, at least in her imagination

TIME
The present

(*An older woman steps onstage, carrying a glass pitcher of water.*)

CAROLINE: Bobby came to me one day, his calendar in hand. He says to me, "Caroline, Caroline. What's this all about?" He showed me the marked out squares and I smiled. "I'm going away for a time," I says to him. "That's my sabbatical." He screwed his face up at me when I gripped his hands. "Sometimes," I said to him. "Sometimes you just have to remember."

I left Thursday morning along the interstate north. To Upper New York State. A six pack of Diet Coke in a little blue cooler and a road map was all I took. All the way there, I counted the reminders.

When I was four, the rain tore open the sky and splashed onto my parched face, onto the squealing animals, onto the dusty ground.

My parents hugged each other, then they hugged me, my mother's tears running down my neck and I remembered.

When I was thirteen, the pastor knocked on my door, Bible in his hand, relations behind him, smiling. We went down into the creek and he dipped me back, back into the warm waters of the marsh while my sisters sang a hymn. My white dress was ruined, but I remembered.

When I was twenty, I met my husband in Bostontown. He met me late at night on the wharf, stepped me onto a rented motorboat for two. He cut the motor and showed me the stars, like diamonds to a pauper girl, while the black silent sea rocked us — back and forth. And I remembered.

When I was thirty-six, I'd wake early in the summer morning, watch the sprinklers rise from the earth like moles, spraying mists over the lawn, splintering the early morning sun into so many rainbows. The steam from my almond tea kissed my face, and I remembered.

(*We hear the rushing sound of a waterfall.*)

Now I stepped out of the car, down the path, paid for my ticket, six dollars. I entered the elevator in the cliff and closed my eyes. I stepped out onto the terrace as the tour guide started speaking, and I approached the falls, that Erie River drop, the great Niagara. And I stood on the terrace as the waters gushed over my hair, down my blouse, over my jeans, through my shoes and I smiled.

He reminds me, and I remember.

(SHE *holds the glass pitcher of water over her head and pours it onto her face. Another actress comes up behind her and holds the pitcher as* CAROLINE*'s hands release it, her arms sweeping slowly down to her sides. We bask in her baptism for a moment.*)

GOLDA'S BALCONY
BY WILLIAM GIBSON

GOLDA MEIR *dreamed of a state of Israel from the time* SHE *was 17 and heard David Ben Gurion speak. Now at 50 and a member of the unofficial Jewish government under the British,* SHE *is sent to America to raise funds.*

SCENE
Before the Council of Jewish Federations in Chicago

TIME
1948

GOLDA: So the British have dumped us on the United Nations … And Ben Gurion says, "Tanks I can get in Czechoslovakia for ten million, ammunition another ten —" And so on, till he ends up saying, "I must go, yes. To the Jews of the States." I say "Leave here *now*?" — everything would fall apart. I say, "Look what you can do here I can't. There I haven't been in ten years, but I speak a good American —" Ben Gurion says, "I must go myself." I say, "Put it to a vote." The exec votes to send me, and he gives in. "All right. Go at once. Today." "Today! — my coat's in Jerusalem!" He says, "Don't even go back to Jerusalem." I say, "You want me to go to America naked?" He says, "Whatever helps."

So I flew out that day, in the same dress.

(*Leaves the office.*)

In New York I bought some clothes—off the rack in S. Klein's, you got good bargains—and learned our best fundraiser was in Chicago. The Council of Jewish Federations was meeting there. Palestine wasn't even in their thoughts. These men continued the fund-raising machinery of America for Jewish welfare hospitals, temples—

So I went to Chicago.

(*Comes to the podium.*)

The chairman in that hall said, "Friends, we have with us today an unexpected visitor from Palestine who has asked time for a few words. Mrs.—er, Mrs.—

(*Peers at her palm.*)

"Goldie Myerson."

I said, "I have no speech. I'll tell you what's in my heart. Fifty-four days ago the UN voted to partition Palestine—an Arab state, a Jewish state—thirty three nations for, thirteen against. It wasn't the real vote. Six million corpses crying out in the graveyard of Europe cast the real vote.

"I didn't come to the States only to save seven hundred thousand Jews after we've lost six million. But if the seven hundred thousand in Palestine are killed off too, we're through with the dream of a Jewish people. When the British pull out, five nations wait to massacre us.

"If we have arms to fight with, we'll fight with them. If not, we'll fight with stones.

"The question is what can we get immediately — I don't mean next month. I mean now. Within a very short time we must have, in cash, twenty-five million dollars.

"You have two choices; we have only one. You cannot decide whether we will fight or not. We will, that decision is taken. You can decide only one thing, whether we will live.

"And don't be bitterly sorry three months from now for what you failed to do today."

(SHE *leaves the podium.*)

HALO

BY KEN URBAN

"Halo" is called a pageant, a play of our time juxtaposed with scenes from the medieval morality play Everyman. *The* Daughter *sits alone as* She *remembers her childhood with her older brother.*

SCENE
The living room

TIME
The last days of the twentieth century

DAUGHTER: My brother and I were about nine and eleven. He's older than me, less than two years. Close enough in years to be extremely far apart in life. We decorated the basement. We used to play school, we wanted to be teachers like our mother. We'd grade imaginary papers, make imaginary bulletin boards and paste things on the walls. Dad saw what we'd done one day. We weren't even there, we were upstairs watching TV, doing homework, it was Sunday. He screamed and slapped Mom. Started ripping things down, knocking our stacks of old textbooks over. He wanted to know why she hadn't watched us. We were sent to bed. My brother came to sleep with me. We huddled together while we heard them cleaning, steaming the stuff off the walls. My mother was crying. The whole house could hear it, sound propelled up vents. Then they came upstairs. We pretended to be asleep. All my mom kept saying was: I don't want our children to hate you, I don't want our children to hate you, Walter, I don't want them to hate you. Ken whispered in my ear: I'm going to leave and never come back.

My brother did. I hate him for it. Now my mother and I have to suffer. I'm getting married to a boy I met in high school. My mother met my father in high school too, the same high school actually. Weird, isn't it? We take walks in the park. Sometimes he asks me about my brother. I talk to him about it and stuff, but I don't say much. Eventually I want to have kids, but I have a career now.

(*Pause.*) My brother isn't even going to come to the wedding.

HEARTBREAKER

BY JOHN MEYER

JUDY GARLAND, *46, desperately in need of a comeback—and a hotel room—is on a call to the booker of the Merv Griffin show.*

PLACE
The apartment of Garland's lover's parents, who do not want her to stay, Eighty-fourth and Park, Manhattan

TIME
1968

JUDY: (*On phone*) I think it would've been nice, actually... I mean, this is just a tip from me... if you'd have let me know in some way, or left a note where I was supposed to be staying. (*Pause.*) Well, he wasn't there. I mean so far it's a bit discouraging, and it's kind of... old hat. I mean, I don't know what this whole problem seems to be, picking up all my—I don't need anyone to pick up any bills, I have enough money to pay my bills. And it's usually the policy of any, of any show to, if anyone comes from another town, to pay their hotel expenses just for that amount of time. Now that's the usual way, and I don't know any other, 'cause I'm not a (*scornfully*) producer. (*Pause.*) You know, you're funny. You are. And I'm not saying this in a mean way, it's just that I've heard this kind of... people who are put in the middle, as you obviously are, always sort of say, "You know, there are certain things that are my responsibility and there are certain things I just can't take care of" — and people like myself are always left out in left field wondering what in the hell happened. (*Pause.*) I'll tell you what: maybe it would help me … as a woman … if we would just forget this. And uh … I would like to talk to Mort Lindsey, because he's gone to a great deal of trouble about the music, and … I would just like to talk to him. I would also like to get, nn, the music because we both believed in, you know, doing the show, and also, I'd love you to send me a great big bouquet of white 'n pink roses with a little note just saying, Sorry it didn't work out. And that'll make everything fine. I would like to go away with some kind of grace, and I think you should grant me that. (*Pause.*)

No, that won't be necessary. At this point, unfortunately. You know, people's enthusiasm has a way of getting quashed by a feeling of, nn, rejection, and if you don't — if you don't care enough, if you don't — look wait a minute, hold it, buddy — if you don't care enough IF YOU DON'T CARE ENOUGH THEN LET THE LADY OFF THE HOOK. (She *hangs up*.)

THE HIGHWAYMAN

BY JULIA JARCHO

BESS *is alone, waiting by the window for her secret love, the Highwayman, to come and see her.*

SCENE
By a window looking out on the wilderness

TIME
The present, or never

BESS: I know what to tell you. It's only the truth. No questions. Of course this is where I am.

(*Beat. To herself.*)

— *You could come—*

(*Beat. To herself.*)

—*out...*

Why?

—*I'd like to remind you that the moor is habitable.*

Habitabitable. Habitabitabitable. Hospitababitle. With life forms. Who savage. Someday something will come in and you'll have to go out there.

(*Beat.*)

So I build up my strength. Emergency measures. I smell my skin. I compare it with my other skin. Things like this'll be helpful. Because I know I've been in here since I was born and no one else. And if someone else was here he didn't see me. And if he saw me he's coming back to get me.

(*Beat.*)

Because he would like me.

(*Beat.*)

Would he want me to go, I think he might want me to go with him. I think that's what he would want. There's no way I can do that. Look at me. I've been here my whole life. A quiet life. I used to bring sugar lumps out to the stable. There's a cellar somewhere here, no, a tunnel through, not the cellar, I think there are stairs and there's a, stairs through a room where they keep … beets? Is that possible? Through there, a passage to the stable. I go through there with my hand full of sugar. My hand is dry. Or both. That's how I carry it through the passage, wedged out of the wet land. So I don't set foot out of the inn.

(*Beat.*)

I get there, I get to the stable. There are so many of them. I'm saying this, it's like a pillar of my childhood. I'm not just any one of those little girls. Because these were not a fantasy. They're, they shit and they take a piss, they have spit foaming up, big sour spit, they're covered with scars and their coats, you can't even say coats, they're covered in their skins, is the most you can say. They'll bite, I have the rents some still on me.

(*Beat.*)

I get to the stable, still inside, I have sugar in my hand, that I took from the kitchen. There are so many of them. Everyone put an animal there and went in to drink. When it's the busy season there's fullness of them. And I'm coming down, there's a push-bell the people do when they need something, but then I disappear, I go get the sugar and I go down the stairs into the place and into the place, to see them, to give them the sugar. I don't know how to describe. I said. Filthy. Some are about to die. Some are on their first trip. Whips. They all have four and some have five and some are daughters. Grown-up. I'm here with the sugar. Just here. I put out my hand … a tongue comes down, no, teeth. You have to put your hand flat and not get bit. Big teeth. You can tell the work. Eyes like my dumb eyes. You know what they want, it makes them want it more, they want, they would say — they can't, but — no, they wouldn't — it makes them want, they want the saddle blanket and the saddle, the saddle bags and the rein, they want, and the spurs, reins and spurs and hands high, but even done like that they want to go, they want me to take them and go, and they would be better off to go, says their faces, go!

(*Beat.*)

And I say I can't. Just because it's not. What about wind and stripes? But it's not.

(*Beat.* [HIGHWAYMAN *enters.*])

Anyway he might not come.

HOUSE ARREST

BY ANNA DEAVERE SMITH

The play is about real events, using the words of real people. In this scene, "Mirror to Her Mouth," PAULETTE JENKINS *is a very beautiful black woman in her 30s wearing a simple, white t-shirt and pants, no makeup, hair pulled back.*

SCENE
The Maryland Correctional Institution for Women

TIME
Sometime during the Clinton Administration

PAULETTE: I began to learn how to cover it up

because I didn't want nobody to know that this was happening

in

my home.

Ya know.

I wanted everyone to think that we were a normal family

and I mean

we had all the materialistic things.

But that didn't make my children pain any less.

I ran out of excuses about how we got black eyes

and busted lips and bruises

me and the kids.

I didn't have no more excuses.

But it didn't change the fact that it was a nightmare

for my children.

It was a nightmare.

And I failed them.

Dramatically.

Because I allowed it to continue on and on and on.

And that night that she got killed,

and the intensity that grew and grew and grew.

Until one night,

we came home,

from getting drugs,

and he got angry with Myeshia

and he started beating her.

And he just continued to beat her,

he had a belt, he would use a belt.

I'm just speaking of the particular night she died.

And he beat her

and he put her in the bathtub.

And I was in the bedroom.

But before all this happened,

four months before she died,

I thought I could really fix this man

so I had a baby by him!

Insane?

Thinking that

if I gave him his own kid

he'll leave mine alone.

And it didn't work.

We wound up with three children.

But the night that Myeshia died.

I stayed in the room with the baby.

And I heard him,

just beating her,

just beating her,

like I said he had her in the bathtub,

and every time he would hit her,

she would fall.

And she would hit her head on the tub.

I could hear it.

It happened continuously,

repeatedly.

(*Whispering.*)

And I dared not to move.

I didn't move.

I didn't even go see what was happening.

I just sat there and listened.

And then later

(SHE *sucks her teeth.*)

he sat her in the hallway

and

told her just set there

and she set there for 'bout

four to five hours

and then he told her to get up

(*Crying.*)

and when she got up she said she couldn't see.

(*Whispering, crying.*)

Her face was bruised.

And she had a black eye.

All around her head was just swollen.

Her head looked like it was two sizes of its own size.

I told him to let her go to sleep and he let her go to sleep.

(*Whispering.*)

The next morning she was dead.

He went in and checked on her for school.

And he got very excited.

And he said

"She won't breathe!"

I knew immediately that she was dead.

'Cause I went in

I didn't even want to accept the fact that she was dead.

So I went and took a mirror to her mouth.

There

was *no*-thing coming out of her mouth.

Nothing.

He said

"We cannot let nobody know about this,

so you got to help me."

And I agreed.

I agreed.

I didn't dare tell anyone.

'Cause I had been keeping it a secret

for years and years.

And it just seemed like secondhand to me

to keep a secret.

That night,

we went to the mall

and we told the police

that she had been missing.

We told like the security guards of the mall

that we had like *lost* her.

Ya know we fabricated this story and I went along with it.

And we told him that she had been missing.

But she wasn't missing.

So after that

we left the mall

and we told them what she had on

that night.

We got her dressed in the exact same thing

that we told the police that we had put on her.

And we got the baby

and we drove like out to

(*Hear her getting the slightest bit tired here.*)

I-95.

I was so petrified

and so numb

all I could look

was in the rearview mirror.

And he just laid her right on the shoulder of the highway.

My own chile.

I let that happen to.

HYPOCRITES & STRIPPERS

BY KIM YAGED

KIM *is a 30-something, cute, nightclub stripper.* SHE *plays all the parts appearing in this monologue.*

SCENE
Perhaps a bar

TIME
The present

KIM: When you're queer and you come out of the closet, there's a whole support system set up—some magical counter in the sky that goes—Ding! Yeah! One more for our side!

When you come out as having a stripper girlfriend, Mom reproves you. Dad nods in agreement—but secretly has unimaginable admiration and esteem for you. If you're gonna be a lesbo, do it right. And your brother asks—

BROTHER: What bar does she work at?

KIM: Just out of curiosity, of course. The thing is, it makes no sense for parents to have such ill will towards strippers. I mean, *Flashdance* broke it all down for us, didn't it? Nude dancing for the likes of mean, nasty Johnny C., the scumbag who kept trying to get into Jennifer Beals' skirt—no. Fucking Nick, the scumbag boss who's fifteen, twenty years older than you and has a hook up at the only ballet company in town—yes. It's okay to works at Mawby's. Remember Mawby? The fat guy who was always shoving a hamburger down his throat? He's a nice guy, and besides, that type of dancing is art—especially the part where Jennifer Beals dumps a bucket of water on herself. She is so hot, isn't she? And all the girls at the club got along so well. Sure, they joked and teased one another, but we all knew they'd be there for each other in a pinch. Talk about camaraderie, friendship—women coming together to help one another, sister to sister. Don't you want to be a stripper too? It really appealed to my feminist sensibilities.

(KIM *catches herself.*)

Did I say I wasn't a feminist? I lied.

THE INTELLIGENT DESIGN OF JENNY CHOW

BY ROLIN JONES

An Asian-American in her early 20s, JENNIFER MARCUS *is an obsessive compulsive agoraphobic genius who re-engineers missile components for the U.S. Army.* SHE *is working at her computer.*

SCENE
A second-story bedroom, Calabasas, California

TIME
Now, right now

JENNIFER: (*To the audience*) Okay, so this firewall is serious. Have you installed it yet? (*Pause.*) Yes, go ahead, check. (*A "hacker alert" noise from the computer. To the audience. Pause.*) Oh, that's cute. (SHE *types in something and the "alert" noise stops.* SHE *sprays the computer screen with disinfectant. We hear a "blip" noise from the computer. To the audience, annoyed.*) Yeah, I'm here. Installed? Gooood. You never know which one of the big boys might be listening in, right? CIA? NSA? We have to be careful, oh, and uh, yeah, we need to stick to what we're good at, okay? You find missing people, I do the computer stuff. Because next time we're in the middle of an IM and you try to break into my computer, I will send an f-bomb of kiddie porn that will bury itself in your hard drive and spam itself back to every sickfuck pedophile in the world currently under

Interpol investigation, okay? I got viruses that can make you piss on yourself and I'm saying this, okay, not because I wouldn't have done the same thing, but because YOU REALLY NEED TO PAY ATTENTION. It's been three days since Jenny got loose. Every second counts. My encryption cannot be broken. Understand? (*We hear a "blip" noise from the computer. To the audience.*) Good. (JENNIFER *puts on a voice-ID earpiece and starts pacing the room. As she talks she straightens pillows, realphabetizes her books, creates order or rearranges order. To the audience.*) Okay, so. here we go...my name is Jennifer Marcus and I was born in a village outside of Maigon-ko, China, twenty-two years ago and...I'm a girl, duh, and I live in a gated community in Calabasas, California. One of the first things you're going to have to get used to is that I'm better than you. Wait, I'm not being conceited, not really, you know, there's a lot of baggage that comes with it. (*We hear a "blip" noise from the computer. To the audience.*) Not cabbage. Baggage. B-A-G-G-A-G-E. I'm using a headset voice identifier, there's some bugs still left in it, so try to stay with me as far as typos go, okay? Where was I? Right, well maybe not better, definitely not better, just more active, I guess. Oh yeah, and I'm rich. Not super rich. Just regular rich. I feel it's important that you know a little about me, and trust me, okay, you'll need it for the job. This isn't your average runaway case, okay?

JESUS HOPPED THE A TRAIN
BY STEPHEN ADLY GUIRGIS

A public defender in her 30s, MARY JANE HANRAHAN *discusses her working-class roots, an expensive private school education, and her conflict with both.*

SCENE
Riker's Island

TIME
The present

MARY JANE: When I was fifteen, there was this father/daughter dance in the elite private girls' school in Manhattan that I went to as a charity case — slash — financial aid recipient. My mother had wisely arranged for her brother, Uncle Mikey, to take me to the dance, but at the last minute, my father decided that him not escorting me himself might be one of those things that might scar me in later life — so me and my father left our two-family house in Sunnyside that evening, me in a dress my parents couldn't afford, and my dad in his Irish all-purpose navy blue suit with a pair of black socks we had convinced him to borrow from the neighbors. When we got inside the ballroom, I took a quick look around and became instantly embarrassed to the point of humiliation by the fact that my dad was the only father on the Upper East Side that night whose suit pants didn't have cuffs. But within an hour, everyone was calling him "Danny," even the head-mistress, who hadn't called me anything but "Miss Hanrahan" in three years. And he was dancing, and chatting; he had even stuck by the agreed-upon two-beer rule, or so I thought...At some point in the evening, one of the other fathers made an offhand comment that my father took exception to; a heated discussion ensued, and my father ended up stabbing the guy with a dessert fork, breaking the skin. What the guy had said was unimportant; actually, what he said was, he was reminiscing about where he had grown up as a kid and he remarked that "It used to be a good neighborhood, you know, white, now, forget it, I went back there last month, it's half white, the rest: blacks and Italians." My mom's Italian. EMS was called, and the dance? Well, let's just say the stabbing concluded the dancing portion of the evening...My father's justification for the assault, after explaining how he didn't *immediately* attack him, and how he had given the "rich jerk" ample opportunity to apologize, and how he won't tolerate a bigot no matter where he is, and "What if your mom or 'Rasheed from the Deli' had been there?" and how he still doesn't understand why I need to go to that stuck-up school anyway. In the end, what he finally said was "It was just a fork." And he said it, I've now come to realize, with just that same look of incredulousness on his face that Angel Cruz had on his...as if the whole world was crazy and he was the only sane one. I hated my dad for the whole mortifying incident, but the dysfunctional side of me was proud of him—actually I'm still kind of proud of him—and I'm not convinced that there's something wrong with me for feeling that. I had no idea why Angel Cruz had "just shot him in the ass" but I felt something—something—and I needed to know what it was. And even though I was no longer obligated to him as his counsel, and despite the fact that the rational side of my brain was very much convinced that he had, in fact, attempted to murder Reverend Kim, and yes, of course, even if he hadn't literally attempted murder, you still can't run around shooting people just like you can't go around stabbing people with dessert forks, I know all that, but I gotta admit that somewhere inside of me, and I don't know if it's the good side, or the side that I saw a therapist twice a week and went to ACOA meetings for, but somewhere inside of me is a place that believes that sometimes you *can* do those things, or at least *somebody* can, or *should,* and that one man's neurotic is another man's hero, and who, ultimately, can say which one's which with any real certainty at all?

JOHNNY BEHIND THE DEUCE

BY LYDIA LUNCH

WOMAN, *late 30s, beautiful but weary, dressed in tight white slip and '50s-style Fredrick's of Hollywood high-heeled bedroom slippers enters stage right, finishing a cocktail. Soft amber light shadows the stage. Monologue is tender and reflective.*

SCENE
A stage

TIME
The present

WOMAN: You can't save anyone from themselves. You will lose everything by attempting to play savior. You will never heal the wounded. You cannot repair the damage already done by selfish parents, vicious ex-lovers, child molesters, tyrants, poverty, depression or simply chemical imbalance.

You can't undo psychic wounds, bandage old scars, kiss away ancient bruises. You can't make the pain go away. You can't shout down the voices in people's heads. You can't make anyone feel special. They will never feel beautiful enough, no matter how beautiful they are to you. They will never feel loved enough, no matter how much you adore them.

You will never be able to save the battered from battling back at a world they've grown to hate. They will always find a way to pick up where the bullies have left off. They will in turn become bullies. They will turn you into the enemy. They will always find a new method in which to punish themselves. Thereby punishing you.

No matter how much you've convinced yourself that you have done absolutely everything in your power to prove your undying devotion, unfaltering commitment, and unending encouragement, you will never be able to save a miserable bastard from himself. The wounded will always find a way to spread their pain over a vast terrain, like an emotional tsunami which devastates the surrounding landscape. An ever expanding firewall which will singe everything and everyone in its wake. The longer you love a damaged person the more it will hurt you.

They will mock your generosity, abuse your kindness, expect your forgiveness, try your patience, sap your energy and eventually kill your soul. They will not be happy until you are as miserable as they are. Then their incredible self-loathing will be justified by the perpetuation of a cycle from which there is little recourse. Once you enter their free fall, it will be virtually impossible to turn your back on them. You will be racked with guilt, frustrated by your own impotence and made furious forever buying into their bullshit in the first place. Of course the more damaged, the more charismatic. The more brilliant. The more sexually intoxicating. The more dangerous to your own mental health.

I have spent months, possibly years, comatose on park benches, tracking the periphery of playgrounds, skulking through shopping malls, falling asleep in the library trying to capture and trap a fleeting image.

The image of a young boy, at just the right moment in his life, that transient fleeting second when the right amount of natural light falls on the hollows of his cheeks, casts an effervescent glow, a splash of sunlight dancing on the lips, to rebirth within me, at least for an hour or two, that blossom of purity etched deep within their innocent smile.

There's something about how fine their bones are. Under their flesh. The possibility of shattering them under my need. Skin pulled tight around bony joints. The flattering reflection of my own beauty divorced of disease, my multiple sicknesses, a withering away abated. Transformed into a healing tonic, a sexual salvation, vacation from the devastation that has ringed the wellspring of my life.

Not that I could ever forget how much of my life has already been melted away. How much I gave up, gave over, wasted. How much has already been stolen. Destroyed. How many rope burns have left their browning residue around my heart strings. You don't have to fight yourself too hard to fall in love at least for half an hour, 20 minutes, 2 days, a week, with a young boy who finds in you the love they never found in their own mother's arms. And reciprocates it twofold. I'll play Mommie. I need to and I'm good at it. There's nothing to lose and what it is you gain is their life force, a transformation, resurrection, a reckoning, a day off from playing wet nurse in the trauma unit nursing damage junkies back to health.

But I'm too far gone now, too fucked up. Broken down, battered. Nothing left inside my angel's saving graces, that busted little cherub with dirty feet and greasy wings whose tender ruby rich kisses have resuscitated so many burning embers and dying remains that I have become a mortician's reanimater, stuck forever in that purgatoid limboessence that so many dying men have come to rub their poison against.

Even my breath has become toxic. An aerosol taint of glue, sugar water, paint fumes, dead roses and runoff. But young boys don't know that yet. Don't see it, can't smell my true essence over the sweat of their own passion. Over the smell of their own vinegar, salt water taffy, dirty towels, steam heat. They wouldn't recognize it even if they did. They have no reference point. No landmarks. No track record. No wars under their belt.

No idea what it's like to inhabit this fleshy prison of blood and bones, entombed as if in an unnamed Nuremberg Cathedral which forty years later still remains swept to the side of a blood stained street, the bones of her confessional stacked helter skelter shattered under the steel rods, the rebar of the enemy pilot jets who blew in one day with the taste of her death on their breath, and in their wake, there she still stands, torn to little pieces praying to be glued back together again.

Praying for resurrection, for redemption. Praying with blind faith and stupid adoration to a cruel and vindictive god that does not exist, that one day the wounds will heal—That a dark angel will tumble down from the heavens, your name on his lips, and with a single kiss, the multiple fractures where memory and madness commit soul murder will cauterize. Will mend. Dissolve. But as with most prayers, I'm wasting my fucking breath.

KALIGHAT

BY PAUL KNOX

SYDNEY, *a 25-year-old Canadian worker in Kalighat, Mother Teresa's Home for Dying Destitutes in Calcutta, admires the skill of her coworker, Brigid.*

SCENE
The modern lodge of the hospital

TIME
Late 1990s

SYDNEY: I don't know how you do the things you do. Like that woman they brought in from the tracks, 'bout a week ago, eh? They said she'd been hit by a train, but it really looked like someone had just taken an ax to her head and left her for dead. She wasn't though. Unconscious, but she was still breathing. And her body was just rigid, like from rigor mortis, but I think it was just from the pain. And this endless, paralyzed look of horror on her face. Her clothes were so … and the smell, well, she must have been laying in the mud there for days. I don't know how she wasn't dead. I mean, her head was one-third gone. And Klaus just pulled her into his lap and rocked her, and Bridge here just started cleaning her up, caressing her hands.

[**Brigid:** What else was I to do?]

Sydney: [I don't know, but] I couldn't move. And oh the places my mind went. And, oh Lord, I couldn't figure out why there wasn't any blood, you know? I mean, her skull was gone from here to here. (*Points to just above her right eye with her left index and middle finger, and to behind and below her right ear with her right hand.*) But, no blood, just this white, I thought it was bone, I guess, but it was pulsing. And Sister Mark came and poured some kind of disinfectant on her head, and this white mass just started teeming, until it broke off in clumps and slithered away from this open crater that was her head, maggots, thousands. I supposed they were keeping it clean, the wound, but ech, there they were, just writhing and crawling everywhere, and these two kept right on with it, didn't even flinch.

[**Brigid:** Well, I think I flinched a bit.]

Sydney: No. Really, she didn't. And Klaus just kept holding her while Bridge and Sister Mark cut away the dead flesh, bandaged her up. And they just sat with her, rocking, caressing, and the horror slowly faded from her face, and her breathing relaxed, and her body slowly lost that terrible stiffness, and she just kind of melted into them and died. It was so beautiful and so terrifying. It was hard to imagine how one could live without the other. And you were able to stay there with it. Oh, Lord, will I ever be able to face my fear like that?

KAWAISOO
(THE PITY OF THINGS)
BY JASON GROTE

An attractive, professional woman in her late 20s or 30s, ELLIE *is also a bit unstable. In her imagination* SHE *guides her ex-husband* MICHAEL, *now dead, through the aisles of a grocery store.*

SCENE
A 24-hour grocery store in an affluent suburb

TIME
Fall 2001, approximately 2 AM

ELLIE: Ta-dah! The produce section! The picture of American dominance, opening like the Emerald City, like the gates of heaven itself. You can drown yourself in pomegranates, in gala apples, in Asian pears. And all that work you did, all that bitching and moaning about the United Fruit Company funding nun-rapists, or whatever—isn't this all worth it? This plenty, this comfort.

Death squads have never been so delicious!

You were so proud, working there. CISPES. Pardon me if I can't share your enthusiasm. I found the counterrevolutionaries as gruesome as you did, but...

Well. I guess not enough for you. Or as much as she did. Or maybe it was just her tits.

(*Picks up a bunch of grapes, starts plucking them and throwing them at him.*) I hope the two of you managed to stop plenty of baby-massacres together. You fucker. (*Her heart isn't in it.* She *stops.*)

This was supposed to have been our big confrontation. I've fantasized about this hundreds of times, smashing a watermelon over your head, force-feeding you grapes—are grapes okay to eat again?—over and over I tortured you with fruit, I buried you in cantaloupes, one time I even put garlic in your eyes—But you—having been reduced, I suppose, to crispy pork skins covered in melted office supplies, and, oh, thousands of tons of dust—

(She *starts throwing grapes again.*) What the fuck kind of place was that for a fucking poverty NGO anyway? You fucking asshole, you smug, do-gooder shit—poking your blond, world-saving fucking graduate student—though I guess she's out of school now—

YOU HATED THOSE WALL STREET FUCKS!

(She *takes a breath. As* She *speaks,* She *starts removing the diapers from the package and taping them to herself, making a kind of diaper armor.*) I should get ready. They were just buildings. They got to us, sure, but if—if they really want to destroy us they will come here, attack us here, where we're safe, where we store our flags and our cigarettes and our nineteen different kinds of water—our greeting cards—That would be real terror, a million planes falling into our supermarkets, paper sale signs tearing as glass windows shatter, the cheap toy machines exploding in a hail of molded plastic crap, for a split second every child's fantasy until the child realizes what just happened, what is happening. Our landscape seared forever.

Imagine how that would look to God, if you believed in God? How beautiful that would be. Pop! Pop! Pop! Pop! All over America. The most accurate map of us there has ever been. (*Pause.* SHE *is now covered in diapers.* SHE *looks at the empty package.*) I guess I have to go pay for these now.

I fear the checkout. I hate to go through alone. It's so cold and ugly, closing the deal, walking through that gauntlet of impulse purchases. There's no cute college boy, either. Just a grumpy old Filipino woman who thinks I'm crazy. Pfft.

KID-SIMPLE
BY JORDAN HARRISON

MOLL, *a very smart 16-year-old girl, has invented a Third Ear, which hears sounds that can't be heard. When* SHE *refuses to sell the machine, her classmate* GARTH *steals it from her locker.* SHE *accuses him furiously.*

SCENE
The finest cul-de-sac of a peaceful town

TIME
Any time

> (*Insert: Sound of rage muted by a thick pillow. Back at the cul-de-sac,* MOLL *wished the cogs in her head would stop turning for once. If only, poor girl,* SHE *could murder her memory.*)

MOLL: Why are you here, you, you … FIGMENT.

[GARTH: Look who's a mess.]

MOLL: Used to be I was your sun and moon and stars. What happened to that?

[GARTH: (*Not too sorry*) Yeah, I'm sorry if that was misleading.]

(*Pause*)

MOLL: I will get you for this, Garth. The world will have to go without new inventions for some time, because all my ingenuity will be directed toward your undoing. I will GET you for messing with my machine and my sanity.

[NARRATOR: Did I mention that Moll has a temper?]

MOLL: All of CREATION will get you. You will be FOOD. A plane will drop you over the unforgiving Serengeti with a faulty parachute, an empty canteen, no sunblock, and when one of these circumstances fells you, you will finally do some good on this planet as recycled material. Your meat will invigorate the ecosystem. Your eyes will shrivel into tiny raisins, the albino kind no one favors. And you will be alone, totally alone, for so long that proximity to another body is *novel.* And when you think you'll never see another human face again, I'll swoop in *deus ex machina,* and say simply: 'Sup.

Your stumpy remains are so glad to see me, looking up to me like a God. But instead of kisses or cool clear water I serve you up a subpoena, bringing to the fore your crimes against United States patent law. MAY ALL THIS COME TO PASS. The loneliness most of all.

THE LANGUAGE OF KISSES
BY EDMUND DE SANTIS

MARA *is a high-strung, headstrong, brash young woman in her early 20s who has been estranged from her mother* ZAN *for some years while pursuing a career in New York.* SHE *has suddenly returned, asking to stay in her old room.*

SCENE
On a farm in Gideon, Ohio

TIME
Late June

MARA: (*Sits at the kitchen table, looks around.*) Wow! Little improvements everywhere! The place never looked this good when Dad was around! You must have a lot more free time now you don't teach anymore. I had a lot more free time the last couple of months. I stopped going to some of my temp jobs. To auditions. I stopped going to. Everything.

(*No response.*)

I had a nervous breakdown. On the #1 downtown. That's the subway.

(*No response.*)

I started having these. Episodes.

(*No response.*)

I thought people were following me.

(*No response.*)

I was attacked.

[(ZAN *stops what* SHE'*s doing.* SHE *turns to* MARA.)]

I'm fine. I wasn't hurt. Physically. Or anything. It. It. It happened in the elevator of my building. This guy, he lived across the street. He was watching our apartment for a long time. Me. Us. He'd go to the roof. Spy down on us. We called the police lots of times. They could never catch him at it. I came home late one night from work. I was doing extra temp work, for the rent. One of my roommates moved out and left Sheri and me in the lurch. I came home and. There he was. Waiting. In the elevator. He whispers, "Pretty girl." But in this sleazy cartooney way — "Pretty girrruulll" ... He had this kitchen knife. He cut my bra open. I froze, I swear I froze and you know, you think you've heard this a hundred times but you can't believe it's happening to you, you think oh, God! has this guy ever heard of Ban roll-on and you see the black sprouts of hair in his ears and nose and oh great the burrito I brought home from Burritoville's getting cold and I'm going to miss Seinfeld tonight and then it's over and ... (*Rocks in her chair.*) He didn't. Penetrate me. He. Came on my shoe. (*Laughs, then gets teary.*) It was scary.

LET IT GO

BY CRYSTAL FIELD

Dressed in her school colors, a YOUNG GIRL *speaks to a hometown crowd set to welcome the boys back home. She speaks brightly and enthusiastically.*

PLACE
Anywhere U.S.A.

TIME
The present

YOUNG GIRL: Hello! Hello all you wonderful friends and family out there. Here you all are. Waiting to see our Soldier Boys coming home.

My Joe is coming Home. It's a good thing. But I'm not supposed to talk about my *own* Brother. It's too selfish. I'm supposed to talk to you about the general population. About everyone else's Brother and Father and Husband and Sugar Daddy and Cousin and Uncle and Sweet, Sweet Child. And I will—I'm nineteen years old—They make a joke. You have to be 21 years old to vote, but only 18 to die. But these Boys coming home today are not dead. And soon they'll be settling in to eat dinner and go to sleep in a proper Bed—With a Down comforter and 200-Thread cotton sheets. Their relatives will kiss them. Some even on the lips. Some will search for their lover's soul with their tongues darting in and out of the dark crevasses of a sand dry mouth. A mouth that cannot speak for itself but a mouth that will revel in the moist lust of a woman, thirsty herself for the sweet, sweet sweetheart who she has longed for all these months...Turning into years now...Into years now with him coming home from his 3rd tour of duty. "Just when you think you're out of Iraq, they pull you back in"...But now, the well of longing will be filled. Happiness will overflow. His weakness will be made strong...Lucky for them, these young Soldiers, they have a mouth to be kissed. Because most of them have lost so many other parts of their bodies. Legs gone, or an arm. A Kidney blasted apart from shrapnel. A spleen crushed between the Rubble from a Roadside Bomb—Lungs filled with Depleted Uranium—Poisoned by their own weapons. Is that another joke?! My brother was so happy to go—The recruiters came to his High School. Softly and quietly they told him about going to College—Living abroad—Seeing the world outside our little little town. And everything's so cheap in Iraq. You can make a fortune just by Buying homemade Rugs over there and selling them here at auction. E-Bay, eat your heart out! But let's leave my Brother out of this. We are here to welcome our young veterans. Our children of the future. Our young, weary, Shell Shocked, disillusioned, dismayed, disenfranchised children of our Future. Minds Blown by the sounds and sights of War. My Brother was at Guantanamo Bay on his second tour. He saw prisoners, naked, with hoods over their heads, attacked by Dogs just barely held on leashes. He saw Prisoners on leashes...Looking just like the Dogs but not attacking...Screaming instead...Terror in their eyes and Horror on their lips. Let it Go. That's what my Brother always said. We have to let it go and greet our general American population Coming Home. Coming Home to our little town—Their relatives are all here. Ready to throw our arms around whatever is left of them. Yes—Most of them are here.

The President says the war is Straining our Psyche—These are Difficult times. They are challenging times. Let it Go—Let it Go — My Brother too — He said "Let it Go." Joe said in his last letter… "Mom please let it go — We are here to protect the President's interests in the Middle East. Our Oil is going fast. I am a Barrier to the Hemorrhaging Black Blood flowing from the Ground. They are stuffing us into the Hole." My Brother's letter was so full of… "Let it Go" he said — "Let it go" — And here I am — I am letting it Go! I am! I'm letting him Go! My Brother is coming home today! He's Coming Home without a mouth to Kiss. Without arms to put around me. Without a moist lust for his girlfriend Tessy. Tessy is here. His mom — His Cousins. His Father. His Grandfather. His Sister. That's me. (*Weeping.*) I'm letting it go — Joe — I'm letting it Go! (*Screaming.*) My Brother is coming home today!!! Hear me Joe — I'm letting it Go! (*Weeping.*) My Brother is coming in a Box. He's coming Home… Dead!

LOLA'S VISION

BY STEPHEN FIFE

LOLA, *17, is dressed in a black T-shirt and jeans, smoking a cigarette. Note: the cigarette is optional. She speaks to the audience.*

SCENE
LOLA*'s room*

TIME
The present

LOLA: Okay, this is the deal, as far as I can figure it: From the moment you're born, from the moment you slither out like some kind of seafood catch of the day, until you're like six, then everyone loves you, you're aces. People come over to your house just to see you, and not just family and relatives, no—strangers, people right off the street, serial killers who've wiped out whole sections of town—they crook their fingers and tickle you under the chin, they make goo-goo eyes at you and twist their faces into horrible shapes. Everyone wants you to laugh, everyone is pleading and praying for you to give them a smile, they are down on their knees like fanatics at some holy shrine... and you just stare back at them, stone-faced, not blinking an eye.

Then when you're around 10 or 11, everyone splits. It doesn't really hit you at first, you kind of wanted them to leave anyway, but soon you get lonely and bored, there's nothing good on TV, you want a body to gripe to. So you wander around in the dark, you stumble and wander around, and whenever you bump into someone, your face puffs up into this big stupid grin, you hop on one foot and do cartwheels, you pole-vault 20 feet in the air and break the world's record, but nobody notices, nobody cares less, and then you look in a mirror and understand why. You are ugly. Your teeth are all bent out of shape, you've got an overbite like Rocky Raccoon, your eyes wander around in your head like kids at the shopping mall looking for Mom ... and your skin. Jeez, you have things growing on your face like they hire hitmen to kill, scientists call up and ask if they can take samples back to their lab. Oh and your body ... oh boy, your body ...

Rashes cover you from head to foot, raw and oozing, obscene shapes appear on your skin like some kind of sailor's glow-in-the-dark tattoo, you somehow manage to look both boney and fat. You learn how to change for gym in your locker, bolting the door from the inside, cramming stuff in the slats so no one could ever see in ... but your best friend Gina, who's a real cut-up, has safecrackers called in. So there you are one day, in school assembly, naked, they've carried the whole bank of lockers to the auditorium, and cameras from all the major networks are rolling, Gina has phoned ahead and told them it was a bomb scare ... (*Raises her hand.*) No lie, that happened. (*Shrugs*) Okay, maybe I'm stretching a little, maybe the networks aren't really there, but something like that really happened, I swear ... It was in the girls' locker room in eighth grade, everyone had already cleared out, you know, I was inside my locker and Gina gave me the "All-clear" signal— (*Mimes this.*) Knock-knock. (*Pause.*) Knock. I could already feel that cool clean water all over my scaly body, when I opened up the locker and stepped out ...

And the whole offensive line of the JV football team was just standing there in full gear, their mouths hanging open, their cleats making a clacking sound on the tiles...and there was Gina, dangling my towel around in the air, and laughing in this way...she didn't even look like the Gina I knew, it was like an alien had taken over her body, all the jocks looked like aliens too, from some planet where people were born wearing shiny white helmets...

And then I smiled. It freaked everyone out, me included...but I was already seeing this scene in my head, like I had visions or ESP or something...How, in the not-too-distant-future, Gina was gonna come looking for me, because some football jock had broken her heart, but she wouldn't be able to find me, because I will have stepped out of this scaly body like an old dress, an old, ugly, pus-oozing dress, and I will have stepped into my new life, as shiny and bright as those helmets...

I suddenly felt really badly for Gina. I knew that underneath everything she was a really good person, and probably the best friend I'd ever have...But sometimes sad things happen to good people, you know?

Which I guess is like the meaning of life...

Which is like what I wanted to say in the first place...

(SHE *hesitates, thinking this over.*)

Yeah.

(SHE *smiles, grinding out her cigarette.*)

LOST AND FOUND

BY DORI APPEL

TORIE *is a graduate student in her 20s who has been interviewing three homemakers of her mother's age in relation to her research about generational changes in women's lives. After carefully dodging questions regarding herself and her family,* SHE *finally reveals the truth about her mother's breakdown several years before.*

SCENE
A house in one of Boston's older neighborhoods

PLACE
A winter afternoon in the mid-1980s

TORIE: I was only there for the prelude—a little kitchen melodrama. I came home from school and there she was, charging around the kitchen at full tilt, throwing all her baking equipment into cardboard boxes. She had a couple of cookie sheets in her hands when I came in, and when she saw me she clanged them together like cymbals.

"Independence Day!" she shouted, and threw the cookie sheets on top of a bunch of cake pans. She was grabbing things right, left, and sideways—all that stainless steel clanging and ringing as one more piece hit the pile.

I said, "Mom, what are you doing?" but she was banging open drawers and cabinets, and by this time she was cursing at everything and laughing at the same time, and she really looked pretty crazy. She'd gathered up all her measuring cups—stainless and Pyrex and even some plastic—and she threw them all on the floor and yelled out, "The measure of my days!" A Pyrex one broke when she threw it, and she started picking up the pieces and cut herself, so now she was bleeding on top of everything else, and she'd stopped laughing and was crying and muttering, and then suddenly she yanked a plug out of the wall and knocked her shiny Kitchen Aid Mixmaster over on its side. It just lay there like a wrecked car while she shouted and beat it with its own electric cord. I was getting pretty scared—I'd seen her upset and crying before, but this was something else, this was like something out of "I Love Lucy"—except it wasn't funny. Finally, she stopped yelling and just stood there, leaning against the counter. There was this little quarter cup measure by her foot, and she picked it up and held it in her hands for a moment, just looking at it. Then she tossed it in a box, gave me a quick kiss, and left.

The rest happened in a motel, but I found a copy of the hospital report in my Dad's desk sometime later on. It called what she'd done a "suicide gesture," which made me think of a shadow play, or something from a ballet. I imagined this silhouette of my mother tilting her head back as her arm floated up very slowly and tipped a bottle just above her mouth. Only a gesture. Nothing to do with death.

LOST AND FOUND
BY DORI APPEL

RHONDA *is a woman in her 40s, stylish, moneyed, and very certain of her opinions.* SHE *enters carrying a garment bag that contains something of substantial weight.*

SCENE
Her spacious and wealthy home

TIME
A few years ago, perhaps the early '90s

RHONDA: I always say that the best insurance against aging is the willingness to change with the times. That's the challenge—accepting stupidity, insanity, and a total disregard for aesthetics.

(SHE *indicates the bag.*)

Do you know what this is? Shielded from view, so as not to offend any rabid politicos among you, I am holding the full length Autumn Haze mink coat given to me by my husband Stan nearly ten years ago. Christmas Eve, and in he walked carrying a huge white box tied with the biggest red bow you ever saw in your life, and right away my hands began to shake, and I said to myself, "This is it, Rhonda.—Think mink!" After I got the ribbon off I closed my eyes, so I actually felt it before I saw it, and I tell you my ten fingers had ten orgasms just like that! Then I opened my eyes very slowly and beheld the most beautiful present I'd ever had in my life! Which in a way was a present for Stan, too—a celebration of what he'd been working his ass off for ever since he got out of dental school. And I say, why not? Why shouldn't we enjoy being…comfortable? Financially secure? (*Short beat.*) Rich!

Well, that's one thing that hasn't changed—money certainly hasn't gone out of style. Look at these kids today—twenty years old and already millionaires. Weird computer geeks you would have done anything to discourage your daughter from going out with five years ago, those boys with no social skills and acrylic sweaters—now suddenly they're buying sports cars and country houses! My son Ronnie has this awkward, skinny friend—twenty-three, mind you, only two years older than Ronnie—who's just bought himself an island in the Marianas, on which he's planning to build an egret preserve! "Ronnie," I said, "who ever told Josh that egrets needed preserving?" (*Smiling.*)

Want to know what he said back? "Don't worry, Mom, the preserve is just a front. Josh is really starting a mink ranch."

I don't mind his kidding me about my coat, it's a lot better than his sister Laurel's attitude of abject shame that she's forced to live in the same house with it. Four thousand square feet in this place, you'd think there'd be enough room for a little peaceful coexistence, but that's never been Laurel's style.

So now I've got an eco-zealot living in my house who treats me like I'm Hitler. When I was her age, all my mother had to put up with was too much time spent on the telephone and a little pleading now and then for another cashmere sweater. Laurel had her own telephone line from the time she was eleven, and believe me I would be thrilled if she ever asked for some decent clothes! I'd happily buy her six cashmere sweaters, but if I brought home so much as one I'm sure I'd have to hear about the exploitation of the poor goats, and the sacrifice they'd made just to satisfy my materialistic lust. That's what I mean about having to meet the challenge of change. I've accepted it, nothing but politically correct fabrics in that kid's bureau drawers. Don't even get me started about the blue silk blouse I made the mistake of giving her for her birthday the year she started junior high. Now I ask you, can any sane person really get excited about the exploitation of worms?

LOT'S DAUGHTERS

BY REBECCA BASHAM

A young rural woman from Appalachia, Susannah Hicks, *whose new husband is away at war, reveals to her sister-in-law,* Gertie, *the sexual abuse she suffered at the hands of a minister.*

SCENE
Eastern Kentucky amidst the foothills in Appalachia

TIME
September 1944

SUSANNAH: Gertie—I have known sin. Momma weren't dead three days 'fore Daddy come into the bed with me. "You got a duty, girl. Your Momma's gone. You got to take on her duty." I weren't a goin' to do it, Gertie. I weren't a goin' to lay there and let him sin on top a me. I scratched and scratched. I bit him on the lip, and then I bit his hand when he tried to cover my mouth. I kicked and yelled and cried and prayed in his face a hopin' the word a God would stop him. He's drunk, though, and the more I yelled the more he laughed. He straddled me, and I kicked hard. While'st he's a lyin' there sick, I run out the house and swore I weren't a goin' back to that house a sin. I ran all the way to Happy Top and banged on Brother and Sister Rankin's door. They made me tell 'em what was wrong. I's 'shamed, so I told 'em Harlen had tried to beat me 'cause he's drunk. They put me to bed. Next mornin', Sister Rankin goes off to town, and Preacher come into my room while I's still a sleepin'. "I am the Lord," he said, "I am your Lord and Savior. What sins have you done committed, girl?" I told him I ain't committed no sin. "I ain't a sinner," I said. He accused me a lyin'. I told him Daddy didn't just beat me, he come after me. Brother Rankin said I's a temptation many a man couldn't resist since purty women come from the Devil. He said I must a done something to tempt Daddy into it. Then he slid into the bed with me. He said, "Pray with me, girl. You are woman and temptation in the flesh. Open you mouth, daughter. You are the child of Eve, a sinful woman let loose in Paradise. Open wider, child. I would rather dwell with a hungry lion than to live with the wickedness that is woman. Suck, girl." He kept a sayin' I's evil, Gertie, and I wanted to pray, but I couldn't say nothin'. I couldn't talk 'cause I was a chokin'. I was "Daughter." I was "hungry, evil woman." I was "Eve's child." He took away my name, Gertie, and now I don't have no face.

LOT'S DAUGHTERS

BY REBECCA BASHAM

Sexually abused by the minister she hoped would protect her from the advances of her own father, SUSANNAH, *confronts his wife,* JOSEPHINE RANKIN, *who could have prevented the incident from occurring, but chose not to.* SUSANNAH *prays to the Lord but directs her anger and her confession to* JOSEPHINE.

SCENE
Eastern Kentucky amidst the foothills of Appalachia

TIME
December 1944

SUSANNAH: (*Keeping her distance.*) I don't have to kneel to testify, Josephine. (*Looking straight at Sister Rankin throughout the monologue.*) I've always walked a narra path, Lord. I've kept to myself, dirty and lonely since I's thirteen so's Harlan wouldn't notice me. I took to sleepin' in the chicken coop after Momma died so's I'd smell so bad he couldn't want me. I only run off that one night, Lord, 'cause Harlan tried to force me, dirt and stink and all. And where did I run, Lord? To your servant's house to be safe. They took me in, Lord, and gave me a bed for the night. Next mornin' early, your servant come into my room, "I've come to help you repent," he said. Then he slid into the bed. He put his hand upon me. He forced me to touch him. He made me pray twixt his legs. He held my head down and made me say his prayer. (*Angry parody of the experience.*) Lord, I take you into my mouth to sanctify. Lord, you are my master and my maker. Lord, I am a child of Eve. I am daughter bound to honor my Father. I am a wicked woman who must be cleansed. (*Accusing.*) You run off to town, Josephine. You knew what was a goin' to happen. You knew.

[**Sister Rankin:** (*Agitated and bordering on hysteria—whispering.*) Hush up, girl! You're outta your head. You don't know what you're a sayin'.]

I know what I'm a doin' just like you knowed what you's doin' when you got dressed and went to town. (*Pointing her finger at Sister Rankin and spitting.*) I curse you, old woman. I curse you for bein' quiet. I wait for God's vengeance to visit you in the middle of the night. Your silence is the sin. You knew what he was a doin', and you didn't do nothin' 'bout it. (*Kneeling.*) I curse you as God curses a liar and a thief to eternal damnation. You lie to everybody—you ain't no Christian—and you help him by bein' quiet. You help him to sin. I damn you to the hell you've done made for yourself. I curse you.

THE LUDICROUS TRIAL OF MR. P

BY SUSAN YANKOWITZ

Spotlight on a woman standing almost immobile. Her head eventually becomes surrounded by a proliferating swarm of bees through which her face can barely be seen.

SCENE
Leeds, England

TIME
1309

LADY OF THE BEES: On a lovely spring afternoon, while I strolled through a meadow in search of wildflowers I was suddenly set upon by a bee, then two … three … seven — oh! I fear to move! — and then more, hundreds more: in no time I am surrounded by swarms of them — I dare not budge, I hold my breath! They seem to have fallen in love with the scent of my skin or the blood that runs beneath its surface; they hum and buzz around my naked face and throat — I do not stir, not even an eyelash! — but one after the other, against my will, they enter my flesh with their barbed stingers — oh! oh! oh! each penetration sends a shock to my heart; I am paralyzed with terror — and still they persist, again and again, I cannot count the number of their violations, but my ordeal is not over, for when the beasties are sated, they invite even their most distant relatives to partake of the feast that I have become. Their venom fills my every pore and vein … A fog swirls into my mind, I grow weak … dizzy … Nothing … will stop them. I see the end … my end … drawing near…

(*A burst of energy.*)

Justice, hear my plea. Take up my case. A life for a life. Do me this last service. Incinerate the hive and those who dwell within. Burn them to extinction … even the infants. For if one member of the family be evil, all are corrupted. There must be no escape for them — as there is none for me. Do this … I beg you…

(*Swaying; fainter.*)

…in pity for me … I can no longer … stand … My tongue grows thick…

(*Speaking with more difficulty.*)

…my … throat is … closing … My breath … breath … a-ban-dons me…

(*Losing consciousness.*)

Justice, avenge me!… I am undone … Done … Done…

MARGO VEIL:
AN ENTERTAINMENT
BY LEN JENKIN

ROXANNE, *a University of Kentucky college student, speaks to a movie actor she has met on a trip.*

SCENE
A train heading for Louisville

TIME
Night

ROXANNE: You know…this world we live in…Look out there…
Nighttime…Stripmall with a laundromat, Dunkin' Donuts,
tropical fish store, tank glows in the window, one huge angelfish
gliding alone and slow in the green light. Turn and turn again
under the cold stars. A vacant lot overrun by weeds, plastic trash
bags torn open and my baby brother squats by a fire, stupid spider
tattoo on his left cheek, blood under his fingernails, dirty piece of
string knotted around his neck. There's the Riverside Motel, naked
people on the sagging beds, full of guilt and fear, fucking away
their troubles in the dawn's early light. Tractor-trailer out of
Memphis hauling chicken parts, driver with a tin funnel on his
head doing ninety down the river road on a twelve percent grade.
High beams on, white light bursts through the motel rooms one by
one, lighting the pale bodies like a photoflash. In the motel office

doorway a man in a Santa Claus suit is sitting on a milk crate. "What you want for Christmas, little girl?" It's still July. I'm visiting my mother. She's in a home, somefuck suburb of Louisville. Highland Park. She doesn't even know who the fuck I am.

THE MERCY SEAT

BY NEIL LABUTE

ABBY PRESCOTT, *a successful businesswoman in her early 40s, has been having an affair with one of her younger subordinates,* BEN. *On September 12, 2001, as the world around them shrieks of catastrophe and* BEN *ignores the urgent ringing of his cell phone,* ABBY *shares her very personal feelings about their relationship.*

SCENE
A New York apartment

TIME
Not long ago

ABBY: It's funny, I probably shouldn't even go there, but — it's comical, almost ... almost comical the things you can imagine while you're making love that way. Facedown. Turned away from a person. It is to me, anyway. The ideas, or images, or, you know, just stuff ... that goes through your head if you do it that way for too long. Ha! Wow, it's ... I don't know. Just funny.

[BEN: What do you mean? ... like what?]

ABBY: Oh, just things. Things that you'd never expect, or be prepared for, or anything; visions that will just suddenly appear as you're kneeling there. Doing it. Having it done *to* you. 'Cause that's what it's like when you have sex that way all the time, like it's being done to you. That it really doesn't matter to the person back there who 'it' is. Just that it — meaning, a backside — is there and available and willing. And so a lot of the time when you're going at it, my mind has just drifted off and I'll think such crazy thoughts … sometimes fantasies, like it's somebody else, a lover I've taken, or that I'm being attacked, jumped in an alleyway by some person … or I'll just make lists "to do" lists for work or shopping or whatnot. I can remember figuring out all my Christmas ideas one night in Orlando at the Hyatt there, during one of our little … on the carpet, as I recall … do you remember that night? We had those adjoining suites … that was a nice conference. In fact, that might've been where I first noticed your particular bent for … well, you know. My *back porch*.

[**BEN:** Abby … why don't we just …]

ABBY: But most of the time I just imagine that it's your wife. Lately that's the thought that I can't seem to get out of my head. That it's your sweet little Mrs. from the suburbs behind me with one of those, umm, things — those, like strappy things that you buy at sex shops — and she's just going to town on me. Banging away for hours because of what I've done to her life, and you know what? I let her. I let her do it, because somewhere inside I feel like I probably deserve it, it's true … and when I think about it, when I stop and really take it in for a moment, it doesn't actually feel that much different than when we do it. Honestly. I mean, in some ways, who better? She knows what you do it like, the speed, rhythm, all that. Unless you do it with her all pretty and tender and who knows what. Do you? No, probably not … she's probably read the ol' *mattress tag* more times than even me, God bless 'er. (*Beat.*) I dunno. Maybe that's what Hell is, in the end. All of your wrongful shit played out there in front of you while you're being pumped from behind by someone you've hurt. That you've screwed over in life. Or worse, worse still…some person who doesn't really love you anymore. No one to ever look at again, make contact with. Just you being fucked as your life splashes out across this big headboard in the Devil's bedroom. Maybe. Even if that's not it, even if Hell is all fire and sulfur and that sort of thing, it couldn't be much worse than that.

MESSAGE FROM THE DRIVER
BY KATIE BULL

From "The 29 Questions Project" by Katie Bull and Hillary Rollins. In this quartet of docu-dramas, the characters present different responses to the event of 9/11. As a whole, the "Project" explores the nature of truth and intimacy on personal and global levels. Based on an actual encounter between a woman and a Pakistani driver, the WOMAN, *a jazz singer, university teacher, and working mom, becomes increasingly uneasy when the* DRIVER *casually asks where she was on 9/11.*

SCENE
A taxi traveling uptown. Borough of Manhattan

TIME
11 PM, October 2001

WOMAN: (*Feigned control, fast and nervous,* SHE *answers to demonstrate* SHE *is not afraid.*) I was at home, my husband took the kids to school that morning. I sat and did some work. I was writing a syllabus for my students, updating it, for the university. I didn't even know it was happening. (WOMAN *looks out the window—her rhythm shifts as her memory pulls her into imagery.* SHE *is alternatively talking directly to* DRIVER, *then drawn back to the images of that day—looking toward the front window or the side window of the taxi, following the images. Acknowledging his presence, drifting back and forth between past and present.*) My husband called me. He just said, two planes hit the World Trade Center, they think it's terrorism. Stay where you are, I've got the kids. They were at school. But their school is on 13th Street. So they were really downtown, and the subways were shut down. God, it was so scary. (*Pause.*) We didn't know what was coming next. (*Pause.*) I went to the TV, and there it was. The first tower, black smoke billowing. And I knew it would fall right then and there. And then the doorbell rang. It was the phone guy. (*Laughs at the absurdity.*) There to fix the second jack. And I just looked at him, he has a friend with him, this woman. And we all just said, oh my God. And we all stood and watched TV. And I said, it's going to fall. And he said, no way. And I said, yes it is. And then it did. He said, it's like a movie, and I said, God, it's not a movie. And I talked to my husband again, before the satellites went down — he was at this friend of ours' house, a mother and father of one of my daughter's classmates. The father is a former fireman. He has a construction company now. He was already going down there. He lived. He injured himself. But the satellites went down. I didn't know what was happening. But they came home later when the train lines went back up. I have never hugged like that. Never been so grateful.

(*Silence.* WOMAN *is nearly overwhelmed by the memory. Then her focus shifts and* SHE *looks at him quite intently. Silence.*)

WOMAN: (*Cautiously.*) And you? Where were you?

MISS WITHERSPOON

BY CHRISTOPHER DURANG

VERONICA *is a smart, but worried woman, in her mid-40s to late 50s. Maybe* SHE *once worked in publishing. There is a sad undercurrent about her. Her nickname is Miss Witherspoon.*

SCENE
SHE *is standing in a pool of light, and speaks to the audience.*

TIME
The present

VERONICA: Well, I'm dead. I committed suicide in the 1990s because of Skylab. Well not entirely, but it's as sensible an explanation as anything. Most of you don't remember what Skylab was ... I seem to have had a disproportionate reaction to it, most people seemed to have sluffed it off.

Skylab was this American space station, it was thousands of tons of heavy metal, and it got put up into orbit over the earth sometime in the seventies.

Eventually the people on board abandoned it, and it was just floating up there; and you'd think the people who put it up there would have had a plan for how to get it back to earth again, but they didn't. Or the plan failed, or something; and in 1979 they announced that Skylab would eventually be falling from the sky in a little bit—this massive thing the size of a city block might come crashing down on your head as you stood in line at Bloomingdale's or sat by your suburban pool, or as you were crossing the George Washington Bridge, etc., etc.

Of course, STATISTICALLY the likelihood of Skylab hitting you on the head—or rather hitting a whole bunch of you on the head—statistically the odds were small.

But I can't live my life by statistics.

And the experts didn't think it through, I guess. Sure, let's put massive tonnage up in the sky. I'm sure it won't fall down. Sure, let's build nuclear power plants. I'm sure we'll figure out what to do with radioactive waste eventually.

Well, you can start to see I have the kind of personality that might kill myself.

I mean throw in unhappy relationships and a kind of dark depressive edge to my psychology and something like Skylab just sends me over the edge.

"I CAN'T LIVE IN A WORLD WHERE THERE IS SKYLAB!"—I sort of screamed this out in the airport as I was in some endless line waiting to go away to somewhere or other.

So I died sometime in the nineties. Obviously it was a *delayed* reaction to Skylab.

So I killed myself. Anger turned inward, they say. But at least I got to miss 9/11.

If I couldn't stand Skylab, I definitely couldn't stand the sight of people jumping out of windows. And then letters with anthrax postmarked from Trenton. And in some quarters people danced in the streets in celebration. "Oh, lots of people killed, yippee, yippee, yippee." God, I hate human beings. I'm glad I killed myself.

You know, in the afterlife I'm considered to have a bad attitude.

And apparently I'm slated to be reincarnated and come do this horrible thing again.

Why can't I just be left alone to fester and brood in my bodiless spirit state? Who says spirits have to be clear and light and happy? So what if my aura looks like some murky brown tweed suit? So what? Leave me alone and I'll leave you alone.

Anyway, they tried to force me back onto earth in 2002 or so, and before I knew it my spirit was starting to reincarnate, but I put on some sort of spiritual otherworldly emergency brake system that I seem to have, and the whole process came to a grinding halt, and I simply REFUSED to reincarnate.

"What if I marry Rex Harrison again???" I said to them. Or maybe next time he'll be my mother and I'll get so frustrated maybe I'll go off the deep end and commit matricide. Or then there will be more Skylabs. And of course terrorism and anthrax and smallpox and monkey pox and a pox on everybody's houses. So no thank you.

Yes, I was married to Rex Harrison. He had several wives so you'll have to do research to figure out which one I was.

I really don't want to come back. I just find too much of it all too upsetting.

So I'm refusing to reincarnate, at least as much as I can. I didn't like being alive, I don't trust it. Plus, you know, if I can keep thwarting these attempts to reincarnate me, I'm not sure the earth is going to still be there, so if I stall long enough, my going back may become a moot point.

(*Looks at the audience, realizes what* SHE *said.*)

I'm sorry, am I depressing everyone? I'm depressing myself. Well, pay no attention, I'm just a gloomy dead person, there's no accounting for my moods, I guess I was bipolar in life, and I still am out here in the afterlife.

Is there anything positive to leave you with?

(*Tries to think of something positive, has trouble thinking of anything; then tries this as a positive wish.*)

Well, good luck. I mean it sincerely. I guess life has always been scary — Hitler was scary, I was a child then; and we all expected to die from Russia and America aiming missiles at one another, and that didn't happen. So good luck — maybe it'll be all right. I hope it will. I just don't want to come back, but if I hear it all has worked out a bit better than we expected, well, I'll be glad. So long.

MOTHER TO SON

BY WINTER MILLER

In Darfur, Sudan, more than 400,000 black Africans have been murdered as the government of Sudan arms the Arab Janjaweed or "devils on horseback," to enforce genocide. More than two million Darfuris are displaced in refugee camps. This stand-alone monologue was written for Eve Ensler's 2006 V-Day activities.

SCENE
A mother cradles her newborn

TIME
The present

MOTHER: One day, I know already to expect it, you will lay your curly head in my lap and ask, "Why am I not named for my father?" And I will wrap you in beautiful lies. Yes, I will tell you my husband was everything to me, the night sky specked with the most dazzling stars. I will tell you he was the desert, dusty and immense. I will tell you his love scorched and burned like the sun. I will tell you an army of men on horseback kicked my husband to the ground and shot him seven times. The first was in the leg, so he could not run. The second was in his groin so he could not spread his seed. The third in his heart so he could not love. The fourth in his heart so he could not breathe. The fifth in his heart to hear him cry for mercy. The sixth in his heart to silence him. The seventh was in the middle of his forehead, for good measure.

But listen my son, for these are words I have never spoken and I will never speak them again so long as I live.

Your father, all six of him, dragged me through dust, my head bobbing over stones. When my dress tore, just as I would, he gripped my hair, pulling me like a fallen goat. Your father, all six of him, threw me face down in the dirt. As I choked sand, your father, all six of him, cut my clothes off with a knife. One by one, all six of him entered me.

I did not make a sound.

Your father, all six of him, called me "African slave" as he spattered his seed in me. Your father, all six of him, said "this land belongs to Arabs now, this cattle belongs to us," and slashed my right thigh with his blade. (So I would remember him), your father, all six of him said.

Alone at last, in a pool of my own blood, I looked up at the wide sky above and prayed to die. When I awoke the village pyre had dwindled to embers.

Your relatives are nameless corpses shoved in wells. My home is a pile of black ash and a stray teapot. There is no one and nothing to go back to, there is only going forward. I will not speak to you of the past. I will teach you not to ask.

NEW YORK

BY DAVID RIMMER

In the aftermath of September 11th, a New York woman visits her psychiatrist. MARY, *mid-40s, projects a pleasant, slightly professional demeanor, not unrelaxed. Instinctive bright smile, brisk manner but cheery and warm, no self-pity.*

SCENE
A doctor's office

TIME
The months after 9/11

MARY: I'm unmarried. I live alone in Brooklyn, behind a Catholic church, which is lucky because it's my church. The Church means a lot to me. The priest, Father Barnes, is my friend. He helped me a lot, but I still thought I'd try you...

(*Smiles.*)

I'm Director of Human Resources—Personnel—for a research and development company. I've never been married. I was engaged once. Twice. Well... once and a half. My mother's gone, my dad's not doing too well. I have two sisters and a brother—younger, married with kids. I guess I was just cut out to be an aunt. Those kids are a joy. I always thought I'd—I never thought I'd look at myself at this age and see someone not married.

(*Shifts in her chair.*)

I've been getting panic attacks. The sound of a bang brings it all back. I just—haven't felt the same. On a daily basis. Little things. I get a paper cut every day. Like clockwork. Everything I pick up I drop. I spill—constantly—I'm making my dry cleaners rich.

(*Shrugs; sighs.*)

It hit me a little harder over the holidays. I was with my family of course. Every time I saw my nieces and nephews run or laugh or have fun, I teared up. They shouldn't have to know about things like—The baby was a comfort though. I looked into her eyes and it was wonderful. She didn't know anything.

(*Smiles.*)

I have a little garden in the back of my apartment. I go there to—sit, relax, and think. And—

(*Lightly.*)

this is a confession, Father Barnes knows it too. Every month or so, I sit there and have a cigarette. That's all. It's not the world's most shocking confession. The night of Christmas Day I came home, sat outside in my big coat, lit a cigarette, and started crying—and I couldn't stop and I burned a hole in my favorite plant. I don't go in my garden any more... All this isn't very important in the big scheme of things.

(*Pause*)

I feel so self-indulgent! I've never been to a—I don't know why I'm bothering you. I'm sure there're so many people much worse off than me. The young widows—I think of them and—I didn't get on the first subway that morning. It was packed and I thought who needs this? So I waited and took the next subway. I got out of the station at Cortlandt Street and saw a plane go into a building. People were running and I just ran along with them. A vendor had T-shirts and another vendor had bottled water and they were passing them out and people were putting wet T-shirts over—

(*Covers her mouth and nose.*)

Smoke and dust everywhere. A high school ring fell out of the sky right at my feet. Then at that little park near City Hall, my cell phone rang. I didn't want to answer it—I was afraid—I hate cell phones! That stupid little ring! Not like a real phone—People answer them in the middle of the street— "*Hello?!*"—You think they're yelling at you!—But I answered it. It was Nina Carmichael. She was trapped in a closet in the tower—She went in there to escape the flames and she couldn't get out. She didn't know how much time she had—she just knew it wasn't much—She wasn't even a close friend. That's the thing— I barely knew Nina Carmichael—She was in my class at college but I didn't know her that well. She sent me an e-mail over the summer—I was helping her with the class reunion. We had lunch maybe once. I don't know why she called me. She said, "I can't reach my mother, Mary. I love her. I love my father and my sister. Please tell them— " She wanted to pray with me. "I love you Mary— "Then she's gone. I went and told them. They were so—Who am I? Why did she call *me*? So she wouldn't be … alone … when she.…

NEW YORK
BY DAVID RIMMER

In this speech from "Stepdaughter," SARAH, *17, sits crossed-legged on a chair. She discusses, with her psychiatrist, the death of her mother's boyfriend,* DENNIS, *in the World Trade Center bombings.*

SCENE
A psychiatrist's office

TIME
Fall 2001

SARAH: So, what.

(*Beat*)

You want my life story? I live in Queens. My mother's an idiot. She has this boyfriend, Dennis. He calls me from this bar the night before 9/11 for no reason. What a dick. No, he — He was just like tryin' too hard to reach out or something. He's marryin' my mom, y'know, so he has to suck up to me.

— Hey, I got a dad!

Anyway, Dennis got a week's work in Tower One. He didn't die saving anybody or anything, he was just working maintenance.

I don't know. I guess I liked him all right. Not really.

Marie — my mother — she loved him enough for two.

It was like, retarded — deranged. I come home, they're all over the couch … "Ohh! Ohh! Ohh!"…

They're so stupid. She's pregnant. She's gonna walk down the aisle like this.

(*Holds out her stomach, does a mock waddle.*)

Nice. Same thing happened when I was born. She was 17. She doesn't learn. They've got this new thing now? Contracepton? Hello? And she wanted me to take Dennis' name. I was gonna bail on that one.

Now I guess I don't have to…

I was thinkin' of takin' my real dad's name, just to piss her off. God, she hates him. She says, "Oh *now* he comes around, *now*." What's the difference? I don't miss him — I never knew him. He ditched her and joined the Army when she was gonna have me. I don't blame him. I mighta done it … I see him once in a while. I have to sneak out but — no problem, she's clueless.

He's a captain now. I don't think he's a hero or anything, but he looks pretty cool in his uniform. I got no problem with him   he's just a cool guy, no big thing.

Then I met his girlfriend, she's like five years older than me. Why don't these people love people their own age? I don't date twelve-year-olds. Dennis was 28. Marie said he could *biologically* be my dad. Yeah right, if he was horny when he was 11.

So my dad's been in some pretty mellow places so far—you know, Germany, Alaska. Now, I don't know, it might get a little weirder in … Afghanistan.

So I'm gonna try not gettin' too attached. That's my thing with guys anyway. Never had a boyfriend for more than a day.

Marie's different. She can't live without 'em.

She cries…

(*Beat.*)

The whole thing's pretty weird, I admit it.

The other day I'm in the cafeteria and this girl Lindsay comes up to me and she's like, "What're ya still bummed out for? He wasn't your real dad or anything."

(*Beat.*)

I beat the crap out of her.

NIGHT TRAIN TO BOLINA

BY NILO CRUZ

A play about two children, MATEO and CLARA, who flee poverty, abuse, and guerilla warfare to find refuge in a Catholic mission; here, SISTER NORA explains to CLARA what is expected from her.

SCENE
Latin America

TIME
The present

(*Daytime. Clara sits on a chair center stage. SISTER NORA stands behind her braiding her hair. Clara is braiding Talita's hair, who is kneeling in front of her.*)

SISTER NORA: There used to be a time when the needs of this place were fulfilled, and children like you spent the whole day in classrooms, learning how to read and write. Now there's not enough of us and this place is falling apart. Everything smells of mold. As when things become moldy and moth-eaten. There used to be a time when this building was airy and sanitary, because we had time to scrub our walls and floors. We had time to maintain our gardens, to cut down the branches from our trees and let in the fresh air.

And in the summertime we used to throw buckets of water on the floor, flooding the mission up to our ankles, so the tiles could retain the cool moisture and soothe the heat. Our walls were painted and there were no leaks in our roofs.

Then things changed. No missionaries wanted to come here to work. And others left frightened of the danger. Afraid of getting killed or lost in our jungles, to end up mangled or mutilated by guerillas or soldiers. So now if the alms box needs to be painted, we take a brush and paint it. All you children have to help us. If there's no one to mend the altar cloths, we take a needle and thread and mend them. Do you know how to sew, Clara?

[CLARA: No.]

SISTER NORA: I'll teach you. You know how to sweep and dust?

[CLARA: Yes.]

SISTER NORA: Good. You can sweep and dust the parish. Take a broom and duster from the room next to the vestry. Talita, you take her there and show her where they're kept. Show her how to sweep under the prayer stools. To get underneath the stools with the broom. Dirt accumulates down there. And show her how to polish the pulpit and the altar rails. The altar cloths are washed on Mondays. The candles are also changed on that day. I like to change them on Mondays, because Mondays are dull and somber. New candles brighten up the church and bring clarity. When you clean the saints use soap and water. Not too much soap or you get too much foam. Then it will take you forever to rinse them. Make sure you dry them well with the cloth I set aside for them. Talita will show you. You know, that's one thing I always liked doing, washing the saints and angels. I like to bathe them as if they were my children. Clean their ears and elbows real good, as I would do a baby. And talk to them. They like it when you talk to them. They like to listen. (*Lights fade to black.*)

ORANGE FLOWER WATER

BY CRAIG WRIGHT

A wife in her 30s or early 40s, CATHY, *leaves her husband,* DAVID, *household instructions because she'll be away for the weekend, blithely unaware that, dissatisfied with their routine marriage, he plans to leave her for another woman.*

SCENE
DAVID *and* CATHY'*s house*

TIME
The present

CATHY: Dear David. Get ready. All three kids need to take lunches to school today. I have already made the sandwiches, but the rest needs to be assembled by yours truly. To make matters worse, Gus has early morning math today, as well, so you have to get him there by 7:30, come back and get the girls, and take them later. And try not to fight with Ruthie. If you wake her early enough, it should all work out, and what I have found works with her is to let her choose the radio station in the car and then shut up. Annie has Brownies after school. As for dinner: You'll be pleased to know I have reached a new state of self-awareness and have not prepared anything, confident that you will be taking the children out for dinner tonight regardless of what the checkbook looks like. Have fun! Don't forget Gus has a soccer game on Saturday and Annie is going to Taylor's birthday party. Maybe you could take Ruthie to a movie? (Can you tell I'm concerned about you two?) Finally, and don't ask me why, the painters are coming on Sunday morning and the fumes are not good for the kids, so either go to church—ha, ha—or take them out somewhere. I should be home by 5:00 PM Sunday afternoon. Please pick me up in the north parking lot of the school. The buses will all be in the south parking lot, but I need to go through the building to divest myself of all the accumulated crap these stupid choir festivals send you home with, so I'll come out the back door and wait for you there. Wish me luck! Cathy. P.S. I stood at the end of the bed this morning, once I was all dressed and ready to go, and the light was angling in from the hall, and you looked very sweet and innocent, very much the same young man who so charmingly and insinuatingly complimented my "nice music" so many years ago. I know we get very busy around here serving the three little Hitlers, but please know, if anything should happen to me this weekend, if for some strange reason, the bus drops through the bridge in Little Falls, or I'm crushed to death by a mob of anxious sopranos, please know that I love you and feel ever so lucky and proud to be your wife in this strange and way-too-busy world we have procreated ourselves into. Yours more truly than truly can ever say ... Cathy.

ORANGE LEMON EGG CANARY

BY RINNE GROFF

HENRIETTA, *dressed in an old-fashioned magician-assistant's outfit, is sparkly and sexy.* SHE *is a sassy 1930s broad, who was charmed by a clever magician.*

SCENE
A stage, with a lot of red velvet (like a Magic Show), a couple of chairs and a table

TIME
The late twentieth century

HENRIETTA: It's easy to get stuck. I got stuck the same way it happens to any other person: by accident. I was studying to be a nurse ... hey, I could have been a nurse. One day after classes, my friend, my fiancé, if you're a stickler for details, took me to see a magic show. Boy oh boy, this magician. He did the usual tricks, the usual stuff—billiard balls, cards, ummmnn, cigarettes, the classics—but it was my first time. I had never seen, I, I, I, had never even heard of a profession like that. I was knocked, completely. I was sitting like this ...

(SHE *makes a slight open-mouthed expression.*)

That's probably why he chose me, called me to the stage. The stage! Plus he liked to call on girls in the audience who had their boyfriends in tow. Their fiancés. Stickler. He said pick a card, any card.

(*Whispering.*)

The Queen of Hearts. I held it close to my breast.

(*Full-voice again*)

He told me to sit on it. Excuse me? He provided the chair.

"Wait," he said, "Face up," and he reached his hand under my thigh.

He pulled the card, without looking at it, naturally, flipped it, and slid it back under. Then he asked to part my lips. Okey-dokey. "Open your mouth wider." Yeah, sure. My fiancé's watching this. He took a small telescope and slipped it inside my open mouth, just a bit, just enough to give me the taste of metal. When I laughed, my teeth came down on it. "Careful," he said. "Be careful." I looked into his eyes. He gazed down my throat, saw straight through every part of my insides, and he guessed my card. He guessed my card all right. And that's what I mean by "stuck."

OUR SON'S WEDDING
BY DONNA DE MATTEO

ANGELO, *a plumber in his late 50s, and* MARY, *a Bronx housewife in her late 50s, have previously had an argument. Angelo has a splitting headache, and is suffering from a form of marital battle fatigue.* HE *is seated in a club chair, in a Ritz Carlton robe. His head is hung back.*

MARY, *seemingly having called a truce, gently applies an ice pack to Angelo's throbbing brain.*

SCENE
A luxurious bedroom suite at the Ritz Carleton Hotel in Boston

TIME
April 2006

> (*Offstage. music is playing from the adjoining room; "Stardust," sung by Rod Stewart.*)

MARY: (*Setting him up.*) Nothing like old music, huh?… music today, a lot of screaming and yelling…

> [(*Angelo closes his eyes, and nods. He puts the ice pack on his eyes. At last, a moment of peace.*)]

It's coming from the adjoining room...Maybe the other family finally got here...How's your head, Angelo? Are the aspirins starting to work?

[(*He nods.*)]

Good...I think we just need to calm down and relax...five minutes of peace and quiet...to listen to the music.

(*Casually.*)

By the way, Theresa Quattroformaggio is taking dancing lessons from my cousin Anthony. Do you remember Theresa Quattroformaggio, Angelo?

[(*No answer. Angelo makes believe he is asleep.*)]

She had six kids and one day she overloaded her washing machine, and a pipe busted that flooded her entire basement. Thousands and thousands of bubbles came out of her house, out of the doors, the windows, the chimney. Bubbles were flyin' all over the Bronx. Do you remember those bubbles flyin' all over Van Cortlandt Park...It was Good Friday, April 1980...We were sitting in the bleachers watching our Michael playing in the Dwarf-Giraffe League. He was at bat trying so hard to hit that ball because you were there. He struck out once, and then twice, but the third time...he hit what would have been a home run, and then...he started running...running the way that he can't help but run...his little hands went up into the air, and the other team started to tease him...calling him the F word...and just as he was about to get to home plate, the sky was filled with bubbles, and...instead of running to home plate, Michael looked up at the bubbles, and never made it. And,...that's when his own team, led by your brother Rocky's kids, kicked the living shit out of him...

("*Stardust*" *is still playing* [*and the expression on Angelo's face has changed. Still with the ice pack covering his eyes, water drips down Angelo's cheeks. Not visible to Mary, Angelo is crying... silently.*)]

...and you, Angelo ran out onto that field, screaming... "Hit them back, Mikey!"...and when you saw that he couldn't or wouldn't even try, you picked him up off of the ground, brought him over to me, and dumped him into my lap. You drove home without saying one word, dropped us off, jumped into your Pipe Dreams Plumbing van and rushed over to Theresa Quattroformaggio's... Do you remember Theresa Quattroformaggio now?

(*No answer.*)

And don't make believe you're sleeping, Angelo. I know you're not. Do you remember Theresa Quattroformaggio now, Angelo?... or maybe you remember her more as Tessie Four Cheeses? You rushed to her house to fix her machine...you said she was practically drowning when you got there...the water measured five feet seven inches, and...you saved her, Angelo...all two hundred and fifty pounds of her before she had one of those fat sucking operations...The story was...seven bottles of Johnny Walker Black fell off of the detergent shelf into the flood...She liked to sneak a little drink while doing her dirty laundry...so, there she was, floating around in a five foot seven inch drink of Scotch and water, drunk and drowning in her hot pink Lane Bryant denim muumuu floating over her teased bleached red hair like a parachute by the time you got there and dove right into that five foot seven inches of spiked water that is known throughout the Bronx as The Tessie Four Cheese Cocktail!... Do you remember Theresa Quattroformaggio now, Angelo? Over twenty-five friggin' years ago, so you can once and for all just admit...that on that Little League Day, that Good Friday when you dumped your son into my lap and took off... YOU SCREWED TESSIE FOUR CHEESES because you had to prove you were still a man even if your son wasn't!…

And what you did with Tessie doesn't even bother me anymore 'cause it's all water under the bridge, but what does kill me is that you were ashamed of our son, and too ashamed to admit you were ashamed of him!

(She *starts crying.*)

…And, maybe in the beginning, so was I … so, why don't you just once and for all admit it!

(*Fade to black.*)

PROBLEM PLAY
BY THOMAS MCCORMACK

JENNY, *24, two years earlier stunned the theatre world in her Broadway debut — and immediately disappeared into her parents' comfortable home — a permanent recluse. Her secret, which only her father and a now-estranged young man know, is that in her teens she had a botched abortion — that resulted in a hysterectomy. She does not say that word out loud here, but it's the event she is talking about.*

SCENE
A stage

TIME
The present

JENNY: (*In a spot on a dark stage alone.*) A personal monologue. What I did on my summer vacation.

I spent two weeks in a hospital during the summer when I was sixteen. I was two miles from home. My mother thought I was a counselor at a salubrious camp in New England. I was hospitalized not because I'd tried to kill myself — that came later. I was there because I'd had ... a misadventure. After which my father took charge, arranged everything, and came to the hospital every day. He looked ... folded at the waist with concern for me, and how I would live with it.

To me, it was like being told I have a terminal illness. That news is supposed to be followed by depression, anger, denial, acceptance. I was never blessed with the denial, or the acceptance. After a trembling, self-pitying summer, I came home, and went to bed with suicide. But in my inexperience I could not arouse him: He was impotent with me. The effect on Mama was ravaging, and I knew I couldn't try again as long as she lived.

That's when I truly became an actor. I preyed on plays, like a spook seeking a host.

My father had tried to protect me in the spring of that year—but not forcefully enough: He warned me about my … infatuation, but he didn't make me stop. A firm word—can you imagine my father not being up to that?

Then, that September, he was too forceful: He found me, saw the pill bottles, knew in an instant what I'd done. He picked me up like an overnight bag—he's strong— and seven minutes later I was in an emergency room … being "saved."

Now he is a collaborator, daily, in an improv I detest. Because like all non-theatrical improvs, its goal is deception. To deceive myself?: Love it. But it's to deceive Mama, and that I hate. Still, I know it's the better good, and I have to do it. So, at odd moments I may resent him a little, while I love him. I don't know anyone who isn't resentful sometime. Except Mama. She doesn't resent anyone. Oh but I think she would!

PROPHECY

BY KAREN MALPEDE

A pregnant acting teacher in her late 20s or early 30s, SARAH GOLDEN visits the baby's father, her former student. He's a 19-year-old war activist who has served in Vietnam.

SCENE
Walter Reed military hospital room

TIME
Early '70s

(*Outside a shut door, Sarah leans against the wall, looking quite undone.*)

SARAH: I visited Lukas at Walter Reed. The place was full of young, beautiful bodies with unlined faces, only they were missing one or two of everything: arms, legs, private parts, and a few, like Lukas, were missing themselves. They lay about like detritus on a beach, containers that once were… "Urns with ashes that once were men."

(*Sarah composes herself and opens the door. The room is empty. There is an empty hospital chair, next to it an IV pole and bag, next to the chair is a stool.*)

Lukas? Hi, Lukas, it's me.

Lukas was alone. He had his own room. So as not to upset the others, I think. He was tied to a chair. His yellow hair all gone, his scalp wrapped. His mouth was open. He was drooling. He was breathing through a plastic tube in his nose. I sat down on a stool next to him.

(She *sits.*)

Lukas, I'm here. Here I am.

I took his hand.

(*Silence.*)

Lukas, can you hear me? Let me tell you … Please, can you hear? Yesterday, there was a great protest, Lukas, the best. The vets took their medals and they threw them over a chain link fence back at Congress, right into the faces of those smirking, self-righteous bastards. You would have loved it, Lukas. One by one, the vets ripped their medals off of their chests and heaved them over the fence. It was on television, Lukas, on Walter Cronkite. The whole world watched it. Your friend, John, he had your Purple Heart. He said into the microphone, "this one is from Lukas, who hated this mother-fucking war, and who is in fucking Walter Reed because he threatened to talk about what he saw." He threw your Purple Heart back.

(*Silence.*)

I asked him what he meant, but he wouldn't say. "What the fuck difference would it make." What did you see in Vietnam? What were you going to say? Who did this to you, Lukas? Please, tell me.

(*Silence.* She *gets up.*)

I didn't talk to him about the child, our child. Because when I asked him the question, "who did this to you?" I could feel him tremble. I could hear him roaring inside like the ocean. A wave rushed through him. And, then, there was nothing. Lukas was gone. I couldn't speak to him. I couldn't say I carried his child. If I had…it doesn't matter, anymore. I let his hand go. I did not kiss him goodbye. I was suddenly freezing. The nurse told me it was time to leave. She took me by the arm and steered me out the door. "I've got to give Lukas his bath." Two weeks later, his friend John called to tell me Lukas was dead. I knew it already, of course. Lukas used himself up trying to speak…He wanted me to know.

PROPHECY

BY KAREN MALPEDE

A U.N. worker, Hala, *a Palestinian-Lebanese woman, is speaking by phone to* Sarah (*from the prior speech*) *about the horror of the recent war in Lebanon. As a human rights and refugee aid social worker, she has also worked in Iraq and the occupied territories. Previously* She *worked with* Sarah*'s husband and had a daughter with him.*

SCENE
Hala*'s apartment in Beirut*

TIME
2006

Hala: Sometimes they bury their heads in your lap, even if they are men, sometimes, often, if a wife has been killed. They cry. Or if their children. Grown men. They tremble in your arms. They have lost families, often, sometimes everyone. They were not home when the house was bombed, or when the search party came and broke down their door, that is often in Iraq, or they were not in the car with the rest of the family when it was run down by a tank, or blown up. Someone was away, someone went to the market to find food, or was in hiding, even, so they would not be taken, they come home. They dig. They find, maybe, a hand. I can't tell you,

Sarah. I will not do it, not over the phone, not in your West Side apartment with all those white walls.

I will tell you about the survivors, the ones who remain alive, after soldiers like yours. Let me tell you about their eyes. Their eyes have a look you do not see in anyone else. They are looking, trying to look, from very far away. They cannot believe themselves what they tell you that they've seen. They do not anymore know how to believe. Everyone they loved is gone. The house. The trees. Their animals. Often, they have no photos, even. And they look at you from far away. They are a long distance from us.

(*Silence. Both women are very still.* SARAH *walks toward* HALA, *then stops, very still.*)

Sometimes, I think we are held here by threads, each one of us, by threads slim as the web of a spider, to the people we love, to our children. How easy it is for someone to walk through our web without seeing, to wipe it away with one move of the hand, without ever knowing what they've done. If you cut a person's threads, they go spinning, all by themselves. They are whirled out to the other side of a divide, to a place where there is no one they can touch, there is nothing to hold them. I sometimes think, what makes us human are these threads we weave binding us one to the other. Here, in my part of the world, family is so important, and now they have no one. I am no more a man. I am no more a woman. There are two separate races. We have very little in common, Sarah, I think sometimes. This frightens me. It should frighten us all. They look at us with dead eyes from very far.

(*Long pause in which both woman turn away.*)

Sarah, I am sorry that I took your husband. That from him I had my child, my Miriam, with her headscarf, and her rage. I didn't want this life. I wanted, yes, of course, my child, I wanted her, and Allan, I wanted him. I did. We wanted, he and I ... We forgot the moment, the present in which we lived. I forgot the thread connecting me to you. We had no idea, then, what would come. We wanted to weave ... I wanted strings, Sarah, threads.

(HALA *turns toward* SARAH [*who turns around to face her.*]) I am glad you called, Sarah, I have wanted to tell you this.

READ THE GODDAMN POEM

BY ANNE ELLIOTT

A poet, WOMAN, *tells her audience about the inspiration for a poem.*

SCENE
A stage

PLACE
The present

WOMAN: This next poem goes out to my buddy Marla, she's in the audience right there (hi sweetie) and she really was the poem's inspiration, at least in part; see, we were once eating cheese fries at Nathan's and she looked at me with this huge globule of grody American cheese on her chin—it looked like a little beard, it really did—and I said so, I said, Marla, you look like the cheese bearded lady, and she said, hey, let's go check the freak show, I hear there's a real bearded lady there, and I said hell no, what an awful way to spend a few dollars on that exploitative crap, feeding the horridness, forcing people to capitalize on their differences just so we can feel more normal, just to reinforce how the same all the rest of us are.

And Marla, she just wiped her cheese glob chin off and told me I was full of it: we are all bearded ladies at one time or another, she said, and we're not paying the freak show people to be different, we're paying them to be the same, to be our mirror, like the wavy-ass mirror in the funhouse, where you get to see what you would look like if things had gone very, very differently. And the thing is, the second Marla said this, a big-bearded person approached us on the street, rounding the corner by the defunct Playland, and as he got closer, I noticed that he had *tits*.

Okay, okay, okay, I know, read the goddamn poem. It's coming, I promise. Hey, this is the poem foreplay, okay? Patience. So anyway this bearded person with tits was approaching us, on the sidewalk in front of Nathan's, as coincidental and improbable as that may sound, and it dawned on me that this was *the* bearded lady. It must have been, considering we were at Coney Island, and what struck me as weird about this person wasn't the beard, not the beard at all. After all, she was wearing blue jeans and sneakers and a windbreaker and her hair in a ponytail like any normal guy with a beard, and she was walking around the corner quite normally, drinking coffee in the little blue Greek paper cup like anybody on their way to work—like me on my way to work even, coffee in that same type of blue cup—after all, normal people go to their jobs, with or without beards, drinking normal liquids from normal bodegas in normal paper cups. So it really was the *discovery of the tits* that threw me, threw me way off to the side of normal, made me realize that everything I thought I knew about this person had disappeared in that instant, replaced by a big fat zero. Nothing, a perfect, beautiful nothing, no assumptions, no normal exists, not now or ever.

I'm getting to the poem, I swear. Don't get your undies in a twist. Anyway, the bearded lady leaves, goes to her job, a normal day, and Marla comments that if a gay person marries someone of the opposite sex to look normal then the husband or wife is a *beard*, regardless of sex. In other words, the beard *is a non-gendered symbol for normalcy*, and she's right, Marla, and I find myself actually wishing I had a beard. Not to be a man, or to marry one, but just to have a beard, a long, flowing one like Rip Van Winkle; I could braid it or dye it cherry red or curl it or really *style* it in all sorts of fanciful and indeed feminine ways. How wonderful it would be to be a bearded lady, or any kind of so-called freak for that matter. To embrace it, maybe even cash in on it. To know that truth, whatever it is, the one that only women with full-on beards can really know.

So I wrote this poem, for Marla, for the bearded lady walking to her job, for all the freaks out there, with their freaky jobs — and you know who you are — or you will, someday, if you're lucky. It's a haiku, called "Ode to the Beard I Wish I Had," and here goes:

Baby pearl of cheese:

Moment of pure clarity!

(*Will you marry me?*)

REAL PORNOGRAPHY

BY LYDIA LUNCH

WOMAN *dressed in black fatigues, black military lace-up boots, black beret stands center stage under harsh white light. Monologue is delivered with evangelical fervor.*

SCENE
Anywhere, U.S.A.

TIME
The present

WOMAN: GLOBAL WARNING … GLOBAL WARNING …
WAR IS AS OLD AS GOD HIMSELF

The War is never over…

The War is never ending…
The War is just an orgy
It's just an orgy of blood and guts
Masterminded by testosterone fueled dirty old men
Who are so sexually repressed that the only way
They can get off is by raping and killing the entire fucking planet

And after all Violence is the sport of God
A vengeful, jealous War Lord whose sadism is so immense

That he condemned us all to rot in eternal damnation like
Flesh puppets tortured in his own private dungeon
An amusement arcade full of fire and brimstone
BELIEF IN A CRUEL GOD MAKES FOR CRUEL MEN

So if the sons of his son are bloodthirsty killers
Bent on murder and mayhem
Drunk on blood, bombs and the smell of burning flesh
Painting the desert blood red in an attempt to appease
Big Poppa, that motherfucker, who was cold enough
To insist upon the murder of his only begotten son

IN THE NAME OF THE FATHER, THE SON
AND ALL THE HOLY GHOSTS

They murder in the name of Mohammed, Moses,
Allah, Yahweh, Jah or Jesus Christ
Threatening each other like schoolyard bullies
Who scream MY GOD IS BIGGER THAN YOUR GOD
So be it!
Oh Closer my God to Thee! Closer my God to Thee!
HOLY WAR! HOLY WAR! BULL FUCKING SHIT!
EVERY WAR IS A HOLY WAR
EVERY WAR IS ABOUT ONE OF THREE THINGS ...
GOD, LAND, OIL
I think it's time we got rid of God
It's time we got rid of God
GOD WAS THE FIRST COP
GOD WAS THE FIRST COCK

GOD CONDEMNED US TO WAR
And man, playing God will do what God has done
To terrorize, to penalize and to punish the earth
AS IT WAS IN THE BEGINNING WAR WITHOUT END
AMEN.

Religion used to be the opium of the masses
Now it's the crack cocaine of assassins
Millions of addicts just high on God
Overdosing and delirious losing their minds
God Junkies throwing psychotic temper tantrums
Like little brats who forgot to take their Ritalin
Too shit scared to admit that God exists as a psychic buffer
Against man's anxiety about his own fucking mortality

THE PRICE THEY PUT ON HUMAN LIFE IS DEATH
THE PRICE THEY PUT ON HUMAN LIFE IS DEATH

The need to believe in God is a pathological viral infection
Which has spread like an incurable cancer
Infecting man's ability to reason

MAN WAS NOT CREATED IN THE IMAGE OF GOD
GOD WAS CREATED IN THE IMAGE OF MAN
So he had something to justify his infantile rage with
Maybe War is just menstrual envy…
If men bleed every month as much as I do
Maybe they wouldn't have such incredible blood lust
Did you ever notice that when you turn on the T.V.
To get your daily update from the CRADLE OF
CIVILIZATION
That they never show the women and children
Not sexy enough! Dressed in burkas and bleeding
Starving to death living on dry grass and sand
Widows and orphans marching to the Border … any Border
They never show the women

Did you ever notice that a woman has never STARTED a
WORLD WAR
Is that because we're still so busy playing the victim
Or expending so much energy on NOT BECOMING ONE

That when night rolls around
We just don't have the energy to go out
AND BLOW UP THE KILLING FIELDS

Did you ever notice that a woman
Has never STOPPED A WORLD WAR EITHER
Is that because
WE STILL DON'T HAVE ENOUGH AMMUNITION,
LADIES?
Maybe we needed to go into Afghanistan and Iraq
AND ARM THE FUCKING WOMEN…

Gun drops alongside the rice and Poptarts!
 Annie get your gun … Annie get your gun
Fuck Al-Qaeda talking ALL CUNTA
I don't think we need to stop the violence
We don't need to stop the violence
We need to even out the playing field
Why should the fanatics get to have all the fun

Violence has settled every single historical issue so far:
The abolition of slavery, the labor movement, women's suffrage,
The right to vote.
Violence is the only resistance against tyranny and oppression.
Second Amendment of the U.S. Cunstitution.

Maybe it's time we started to speak to THEM, THE DICK-TATORS
in their own language, a language based on FEAR, POWER and
GREED.

Maybe it's time to turn the FEAR AROUND. Give THEM
something to be frightened of.

I realize that in the past I would have been burned at the stake.
In a witch hunt like the 9 million other menstrual murders of the

Middle Ages.
Now all I can dream of is 9 million menstruating murderesses,
storming through the White House, The House of Commons,
The Middle East, Africa, the deserts and jungles, the desert
screams for blood, let us slake her thirst.

When it's time to kill or be killed, I know what end of the barrel
I'm going to be staring down.

If the God Bullies are so ready to die
For the glory of their Master
Then SHOOT THEM ALL and let God sort them out.

And this might just be JUDGMENT DAY
AND THE JURY'S IN
AND THEY ARE ALL FUCKING GUILTY
OF CRIMES AGAINST REASON
CRIMES AGAINST NATURE
CRIMES AGAINST HUMANITY

The Sunnis against the Shiites against the Jews against the
Palestinians against the Christians against the Baptists against the
Protestants against the Mormons against the Scientologists against
ME who is against all their false fucking idols.

And with the blood of a thousand Christs
I wash my hands of mercy
Divine Retribution would be killing the killers
Who use God as a battering ram
To shove down the throats of those
They consider less than Holy

Ladies, how did we manage to devolve
From sacred prostitutes to corporate whores
From Warrior Queens to pop porn princesses

We've gone from Kali to Courtney Love
From Medusa to Madonna
From Lilith to Liv Tyler
From Emma Goldman to Uma Thurman
From Angela Davis to L'il Kim
From Patty Hearst to fucking Paris Hilton

We need to get back to the Goddess
You know what the Goddess said?
You know what Durga said?

DURGA SAID CUT OFF YOUR OWN FUCKING HEAD
You want to go on a SUICIDE MISSION, GO ON A SUICIDE
MISSION
ONE MAN, ONE BOMB, AND LEAVE THE INNOCENT
WOMEN, THE INNOCENT CHILDREN AND THE
INNOCENT MALE CIVILIANS OUT OF IT.

THE REBIRTH

BY LISA SOLAND

A 76-year-old widow from Boston, DORIS *carries a shopping bag and purse. She is spunky, thoughtful, and, at times, humorous.*

SCENE
A congressional hearing room in Washington, D.C. The audience represents the committee.

TIME
The present

DORIS: You want to know how many people I don't feel like a "little-old-lady" with? None. Not a single one. So I went. I went. And I went.

(*Beat.*)

They called it "The Rebirth." And I thought, "Well, good. That's just what I need because all of my life I've seen endings. A rebirth would be nice for a change." My husband—Max Junior...? Not that he was much of a junior, in fact, if you'd seen him in the private places a marriage tends to allow two people to see each other...

(*Suddenly.*)

Well, he died you know. Just up and died. Sleeping peacefully one night, so peacefully I looked at him, his face right beside mine so closely, so closely that I noticed there was no more air coming out of his nose. That big, beautiful, hairy nose and no more air. What a panic.

(DORIS *crosses to table.*)

My mother's death—quiet, too, on the outside. Not so quiet on the inside. Cancer.

(*Places purse on table then takes hanky out of sweater pocket and blows nose.*)

I thought my parents would never die, says the old, gray-haired woman...

(*Patting her hair back into place.*)

...which I thought would never be gray. Youth. Ha! A little bottle of Clairol can go a long way.

(SHE *spots* SAMUEL*'s tie on table and rolls it up neatly.*)

I promised my husband he would never be married to a gray-haired woman and I plan to keep that promise.

(*To audience, proudly.*)

I'm 76.

(*Singing, and miming playing the trombone.*)

"Seventy-six old bones lead the big parade!"

(*Continuing.*)

And I can't tell you how that happened either. I lost track of the last 50. Gone, like the 50 pounds my mother lost before she left me.

(*Really asking these questions.*)

Where does it go? The 50 years? The 50 pounds? Where did she go? Like light. When it turns dark, where does the light go? Well, these 76 old bones can tell you through experience that when it's dark here, it's light somewhere else and soon, very soon, it gets light again.

(Doris *sits in chair.*)

Death. I was always afraid of it, you see. Because I'll be last. When you're first, you're okay, because you're leaving those you know. You've got them all around you and you're leaving them. They're pretty much screwed but you … I imagine you're okay. But when you're last, you don't know anyone anymore. They've all died, so you leave alone and you enter … what? And you don't know if anyone's going to be there either. I mean, you read the books. They say you go through some tunnel and you leave the dark and go towards the light, some blinding light, but what if no one's there waiting for me?

(*Beat.*)

Sometimes I imagine my mother there, with her calico apron on, telling me to soak my grape nuts before I eat them so I won't crack my teeth. And I wonder about Max?

(*Beat.*)

It's been so long I would think their souls would have all moved on by now.

(*Feeling her loneliness.*)

No one I know will be there.

(*Rising,* SHE *moves to edge of chair and mimes being her mother.*)

My mother's spirit is probably off working on the United Nations council, passing thoughts about crunchy cereal into the shallow minds of our world leaders.

(SHE *shrugs.*)

Who knows?

(*Beat.*)

In my breath work session, I became a star up in the sky. And I realized that that's all they were, *we* were, is bright light, all ashine, bursting into massive expansiveness. I felt very free and peaceful and aware that Max's death was nothing but that—a passing into expansiveness. From his big, hairy nose to the sky in one, short breath.

(*After a thought.*)

I guess that can be kind of scary if you're not ready. Leaving what you know, to go ... where?

(*Really asking the audience.*)

Where? I have no grandchildren. Imagine that. I look like a Hallmark greeting card and I have no grandchildren. The odds were against me seeing as I had no children.

(*Crosses to purse on table.*)

I did actually, but she disowned me.

(*Beat.*)

No, I disowned her.

(*Gets wallet out of purse and shows photo of daughter to audience.*)

Here. See? She was stubborn. Stubborn as a one-eyed mule. You can spot it in the eyes. Just like her father.

(*Shows photo.*)

She kept telling me that she could never burden me with the raising of her child. I said, "What? Your child?! What makes you think it's yours? Maybe it's mine, given to you. Through you. Meant for me but given to you." She said that she was going to abort it. That she had no choice. So I have no grandchildren.

(*Closes wallet and puts it back in purse.*)

I don't mind leaving nothing behind, really, it's not leaving *with* anything that bothers me.

(DORIS *sits on edge of stage.*)

After the tour of the stars, my mind seemed to settle on one, particular incident that actually happened to me, in real life, when I was nine. But I got to re-live it all again, speeding before my mind like a three-dimensional hologram.

(*Beat.*)

I used to love to climb this one particular tree, down the hill behind our farmhouse. I think it was a walnut tree.

(*Thinking.*)

Yes.

(*Becoming the tree with her arms.*)

It had the type of limbs that swooped way down near the earth but it was also very tall. Very tall. When I climbed, I felt as though I were getting nearer and nearer to heaven.

(Doris *rises and, becoming the little girl,* She *starts to climb.*)

One day I was feeling very rambunctious, so I tried a branch that any other day I would have passed by. I just had to go a little bit further. I wrapped my fingers around it and began to pull my little 62-pound body upwards, towards the sky. Mid-way, I saw a little, tiny crack starting to form in a place of the branch that mattered. I was aware that it was about to give way and it sure enough did. I fell. My mother's warnings flashed through my mind and I wished I'd listened to her just this one time 'cause I was a good five stories about the ground.

(*To audience.*)

Now, this is the part I didn't remember until the breath work. I must have blocked it out or something, but I knew I was going to hit hard, so I left. I left my body. And right then, as I made that instant decision, I reached my hand upwards, and there was my father, reaching down out of heaven.

(*To audience.*)

I hadn't seen him in years. He had died of liver disease when I was six but here he was catching me, midfall. I smiled at him and he asked me in his mind, without speaking, why I hadn't listened to my mother. I told him that she often tried to keep me from doing things that I had an enormous curiosity about. Without speaking again, he said that I would now have to make my own decisions in life, about what was safe and what was not. And I cried.

(*A very bright light slowly comes up full on* Doris.)

I remember crying but not because of the fact that I was now going to have to grow up, but because my father was lit up like a candle on Christmas Day, so bright I could hardly look at him.

(*Becoming the child again.*)

All the stories my mother tried to paint for me about him throwing things, drinking, could not have possibly been true 'cause there was my daddy. He was there, in heaven.

(*Continuing the story.*)

He cradled me in his arms and pointed to the ground below, where my physical body lay, knocked out flat and said, "You've got your whole life waiting for you down there. Are you ready for it?"

(*Beat.*)

I wrapped my legs around his stomach and the next thing you know, I'm lying on the ground with a splittin' headache that could have killed a plow horse.

(*Poignantly.*)

My mother died later that same month.

(*Beat.*)

That was my first experience with this light when I was six and I got to remember it in my breath work. The same light that surrounded my father that day will lead me down that tunnel. But not because I'm going to fall from a tree…

(*Plainly to audience.*)

…because I'm going to die.

(SHE *gathers her purse and shopping bag.*)

Well, I'm old and that's the way life is. People don't want to hear it, but it's true. Despite all my positive thoughts on the subject and Deepak Chopra…I am still going to die. Not quite yet, however. Part of me thinks it sucks and part of me accepts it. And I bounce back and forth between the two about 76 times a day.

(*Singing and miming playing the trombone.*)

"76 old bones…" I have noticed however, since I've been doing these sessions that I accept it more times than naught. And that's a real blessing.

(*Crossing downstage to audience.*)

Spending time with you young people helps too, because you have so much life in you—so much…living left to do that it reminds me of dying. Sounds like a dichotomy, doesn't it?

ROCK THE LINE

BY KATHLEEN WARNOCK

A crowd has been waiting for hours in the parking lot to see a rock concert. Candy, *a seriously messed-up druggie, returns from the restroom, wiping her mouth with her hand.*

SCENE
The parking lot

TIME
The present

Candy: Hey … you gotta light? Why? Are you a pussy? You afraid of cancer? You afraid of me? Afraid you'll *catch* something?

I was in a band called Candy File and the Travelers. We opened for Patti. She said I was good. She said I rocked. It was at the Whisky a Go Go in L.A., on the "Don't Fuck With Mother Nature" tour … I went to the club and gave them our tape, and I called and I went there every day. And my band thought I was nuts. But we got booked. We were opening for Patti fucking Roxx! I made us practice till our fingers bled. Till we had to glue the calluses back on. Played rhythm, of course. A '57 Les Paul. Rock like the earth is made of. Rock that breaks windows and slides down mountains and crushes houses. ROCK. Punk ROCK. Like Iggy. The Sex Pistols. The

Damned. Th Dictators. I WROTE "Rock the Casbah." I WROTE "I Wanna Be Sedated." I WROTE "Beat on the Brat."

IT'S NOT THE RAMONES!

That's what it SAYS on the credits...you don't know the record industry. You don't know the rip-offs and the scams. Are you questioning me? Are you doubting my veracity? I wanted to take my guitar and lay it at Patti's feet and have her bless it. I wanted the word. The Okay. The high sign.

When we hit the stage the crowd started screaming...you never saw anything like it. They were fighting and grabbing me, and I clocked one guy with my guitar, and kicked another one in the face, and I said: are you ready to rock motherfuckers? And it was like the fuckin' end of the world! It was hot and red likes the fires of hell, I was pouring sweat, and I was singing like an archangel, and they were screaming. At the edge of the stage there was Patti. She was rocking out to ME. ME. I was Candy. I was Patti. I was US. We were both Me. I could feel her energy possessing my body, and her voice coming out of my mouth, and I WAS HER! And when we left the stage, I went down, I was so empty. And I felt this pair of arms around me ... it was Patti ... and she pulled me up and said: get back out there. It was the night I should have died, man ... because ... there wasn't anything after. That was all I ever wanted to be. (*Pause.*) She invited me to hang out. We partied. We smoked a joint. We rode in her limo around Hollywood and we drank champagne. And at the end of the night, she dropped me off at my place, and said, hey man, you're good. Keep on rocking. She said she would see me around. And I went home. And it was the same. There were cracks in the ceiling, and roaches in the kitchen, and a mattress on the floor, and people screaming...screaming to me. I knew I had to get out of there, I had to get to Patti. Patti started talking to me. She told me she wanted me. She told me to be with her.

I heard from her. I heard from her every day, every minute. I called her office, and her record company. I wrote her letters, I quit my band and started following the tour.

YOU DON'T UNDERSTAND! She CAME to me, in my bed at night, and in my dreams. Her management tried to keep me from getting to her, but she knows I'm there. She sends me messages in the songs. (SHE *pulls out a knife.*) I see you WATCHING me. I see you JUDGING me. Don't you fuckin' feel sorry for me. I'm going to remember you. I'm keeping an eye on you tonight, pussy. She talks to me! Patti!

SANS-CULOTTES
IN THE PROMISED LAND
BY KIRSTEN GREENIDGE

An attractive black woman of 25, Lena *works as a nanny for* Greta *in an affluent black household. Not by any means stupid,* She *is unable to read, and the secret jeopardizes her employment.* Lena *speaks to* Charlotte, *a black activist teacher.*

SCENE
On a park bench

TIME
The present

Lena: The principal's son was my sweetheart: so I got my diploma: I wasn't one of those drop-outs that smoke behind the Walmart. I found my way. I'm not stupid: I pay attention. I had a teacher who was real into words, real into saying words the right way. I paid close attention to every little thing she said, and it worked: I don't sound like one of those people on the T.V. who can't put a sentence together, can't hardly talk: I'm not stupid. I keep up with everything. Even my bills. Each bill I get I send to my grandmother in Fort Worth. Over the phone she tells me how to make out my checks. The only problem right now is that washing machine. Greta's going to be walking around in rags if I don't tell them about me soon. People usually understand after I explain, after I tell them that letters don't work for me. Letters twist around before my head gets a chance to figure them out. People usually understand, but sometimes, sometimes they don't. That's … that's what happened at my last place. The mother there would write me things. I was really good at figuring them out except this one time, my last time, I wasn't, so good. It was a birthday party. I was supposed to take her two girls to this birthday party. She wrote the directions on this piece of paper. Easy, I thought. I just get the big one to read it, say my eyes hurt, or I forgot my glasses. I got a whole list of things I can say. And I can drive okay but directions, when they're on paper like that, are no good. So I stay calm. I drive around for a little. I wait. I drive a little more, then I make a joke: I say "Hey, make yourself useful." I give a little laugh, too, to go with the joke. But the big one, the ugly one with the big teeth she says "No." Just "No" flat out like that. She says it's not her job, it's mine. She says it's what her mother pays me good money for. So I ask the little one, I don't get huffy I just ask the little one if she can read. But. She can't. So I drive. Around and around 'til they both fall asleep. Big teeth and her sister. Useless. I drive thinking maybe I'll see a house with balloons. But I don't. Next day the agency calls. They say don't go to work today. They say I get one more chance before they have to let me go. This is my one more chance but that Carrmel's creeping around spying on me and the mother keeps writing me notes. How am I supposed to keep my job if she writes me notes?

SCENES FROM
AN UNFINISHED LIFE
BY LEIGH KENNICOTT

A young, unmarried GIRL *contemplates her choices after discovering she is pregnant.*

SCENE
GIRL*'s bedroom*

TIME
The present

GIRL: A kid out of wedlock? Finding baby sitters while I work at a job, not a career. Finding day care. And no more dating. Colds. Measles. Chicken pox. Lower paying jobs, just to keep flexible. Moving to escape the stigma. Moving to find the best schools. Finding the money for dancing lessons. Or piano lessons. (I know it'll be a girl.) Enduring angry teenagers. No dates. Making the poor thing excel just so it can get into a good college 'cause I won't be able to pay. Grey-haired at graduation. It becomes a drug addict. Or worse. And no dates.

I certainly sound confident, don't I? In reality, I'm scared stiff. And now the guy who threatened to break up with me if I didn't go to bed with him—he's disappeared. I can't turn to my parents. How do I know so much about how horrible it is to raise children? From my mother, who never ceases to complain about how Motherhood ruined her career.

(SHE *thinks a moment.*)

Abortion doesn't seem like an option. They're almost illegal. And how do I find one? It seems as though I have two choices: go far, far away and have it, depending upon the mercy of strangers—or suicide.

(*A significant pause.*)

I'll choose suicide.

SECOND.

BY NEAL UTTERBACK

A tough, no nonsense reporter, in her late 20s, VICK *has just returned from a frustrating assignment. She enters in a huff.*

SCENE
The New York apartment of VICK *and her partner*

TIME
Christmas

VICK: This assignment. My God. The crap they will send me on. Have you been following this? I am an award-winning journalist, for Chrissake. So, this guy — have you been watching the news? Some bum, some homeless guy — or maybe he's not, no one knows — this guy, claims to be the Second Coming of… well, no, he's not claiming it. Everyone *else* is claiming it. (SHE *briefly exits to remove her jacket.*) He's not saying anything. No one can even find him. You didn't hear about this? It all started like two weeks ago. (SHE *returns.*) This old lady is walking down Eighth Avenue. Meanwhile, this cop car is giving chase to some criminal … a car chase — in Manhattan — in December. The cars whip onto Eighth, the lady is walking cautiously because of the ice, the first car hits the ice, careens out of control, SMACK, right into grandma. She goes flying like ten feet onto the pavement. Head cracked

ing

wide open, blood everywhere. (*Clearly still too warm or too cold or…something,* SHE *goes back to change, talking all the while.*) The driver regains control. The cops race after the other car. A group of people converge around the victim, they call 911, they're frantic, "Oh my God, what do we do, blah blah blah." And from out of the crowd comes this youngish looking, attractive or maybe not, white, African-American or Hispanic, male with dark hair or wearing a ski cap who may or may not have a beard depending on who you ask—but he's clearly down on his luck, ratty clothes, a bum. (SHE *returns wearing a colorful robe.*)

This guy comes out of the crowd, kneels down by the woman, lays his hand on her head, and— (SHE *snaps her finger*s.) —she's fine, a little dazed but fine. Then the Miracle Man vanishes somehow—evangelical evanescence—in a crowd of New Yorkers—not a word from him, no one stops him. *And.* Although, we live in an age of palm-sized video recorders, of reality TV home movie bloopers, of cell phone cameras, for the love of God—does anyone get a picture of our hero? NO. They all, all twenty-two of them that stuck around, gave a vaguely similar description, which gave us this. (SHE *holds a copy of a* New York Times *front page story—which remains on stage for the entire play—of the "Miracle Man" with an artist's rendering of a nondescript man.*) Who is this? This could be anyone. This could be my accountant brother in Connecticut. But they all claim they have seen a miracle. Maybe, maybe even, the Messiah. Amazing, you say? No. It's ridiculous. I mean, if you ask me, the real miracle is getting twenty-two New Yorkers to believe such a preposterous thing. And he can't be found. No one is coming forward—or rather everyone is coming forward saying they are sure their neighbor is "the Miracle Man," or "Saint Nicholas," or "Captain Christmas" if you work for the *Post.*

But you know what it is? It's Prescott, that prick. He's afraid of me. He's afraid and he's determined to sabotage my career and my credibility and take me out of the running for his job, which I am in. So, on some level I have to respect that fat, sweaty troll bastard. But that smarmy creep has a second thing coming, believe you me. I will get his job and run him out of the business and the tri-state area. (SHE *goes to get a glass and returns.*) And then there's this Armageddon blizzard. You're lucky your plane even made it in. Another hour and no way, baby. Henry is calling for it to be the worst storm in *recorded history*. Of course, Henry doesn't know the first thing about the weather. They only keep him on because he's older than Moses. Prescott, as God as my witness, he's actually moist. His skin has this… it's like his parents hawked up a loogie and christened it. (SHE *pours a glass of wine.*) Oh, *and*, of the twenty-two people who stuck around and gave their names, half of them are hookers, drug addicts, or criminals themselves. These are my sources? They're no help. I tried interviewing one guy, who I tracked, I swear to God, into an abandoned warehouse. He couldn't get through an entire sentence without having some kind of (VICK *begins jerking in spasms.*) fit.

THE SECRET OF LIFE
BY DAVID SIMPATICO

In this first of the play's monologues, IRENE, *who works in a deli making sandwiches, discovers that her customer is a long-lost friend from high school.*

SCENE
A deli counter

TIME
The present

(*The lights come up on Irene, working behind the counter of a gourmet deli. At first glance* SHE *is calmly attractive, with an air of average existence about her. However, the delicately wrought bands of silver around her wrist and the deeply etched lines beneath her eyes tell us* SHE *has a depth of experience far beyond the average. As* SHE *wipes her hands and turns to face her new customer,* SHE *is struck with a momentary blast of sudden recognition; standing across the counter from her is her best friend from Before Tenth Grade. The happy shock sends Irene off on a non-stop express train of kaleidoscopic needs. Throughout the monologue,* SHE *addresses the audience as if the whole room were her long-lost friend.* SHE *makes a sandwich, but, by the end, only gets so far as cutting open the roll.*)

(*Wiping her hands clean, repeating an order to a customer without looking at him.*)

IRENE: Uh huh Uh huh Uh huh Uh huh got it got it let me see now ham, cheese, salami, tomato, lettuce, pickle, onion on rye excellent did you want some nice Grey Pou —

(*Suddenly recognizing the customer — (the audience) — from out of her own past.*)

Oh my God Oh my God Oh my God Oh my God I cannot believe it this I cannot believe I mean can you believe this I mean this is insane, I mean, my God, how are you, I mean I just can't believe it's you because I was thinking about you all morning and I was actually trying to remember something else but you just kept popping up and what, the last time we talked was what, tenth grade correct me if I'm wrong here Driver's Ed, right, so oh my God what did you say, oh wait, that's right, wait a minute ham, cheese, salami, tomato, lettuce, pickle, onion on rye but listen, I just got these Kaiser fresh, so how's I do you a little favor just for old times sake and you like Kaiser, right, I remember, my God, I mean you could have gone across to the Korean, but you didn't because they call that like karma, I mean I don't know what the Koreans call it but somebody calls it karma, I mean I knew who it was immediately I mean it's in your spine that's where it is, that's who you are, my God look at me I can't stop talking you got me so excited I thought I'd never see you again I mean I've been waiting so long I was on the verge of giving up hope you know, I mean what the last time was what, that film in Driver's Ed about cars that crash and burn, and then I was out of there for good but I never forgot about you and I always looked for you no matter how scared I was that maybe my life was floating past me like little pieces of bad wood going down-river over the falls to the bottom of the pit right, I mean I was doing 130 with my eyes shut cruising all over the place making tons of money because believe me one thing leads to another and I had this fabulous blood-red Spider and this fabulous life in this fabulous apartment on fabulous Fifth Avenue playing Party Girl of the Fabulous Planet vibrating at fabulously high speeds going faster and faster and Europe and Tibet and Hong Kong where dog is a delicacy and burning up Page Six and smiling and vibrating and smiling and do you remember eighth grade biology with Mr. Spagnola and soaking the cloth in ether and the live frog and pinning it to the piece of wood and dissecting it for a good grade and the poor little frog was still alive but couldn't move because of the pins and couldn't scream because of the ether but could still feel the scalpel and just had to stay there pinned into the wood unable to do anything but wait to die from the pain?

(She *puts the knife in the roll.*)

That was me. I was that frog.

SEPARATION ANXIETY

BY JUNE RIFKIN

A woman, Ruby, is reflecting on her life on the eve of her divorce. The ghost of her deceased grandma, Pearl, who was a Rockette, comes to visit her to give Ruby a pep talk about how tomorrow will be a new beginning and she can persevere.

SCENE
Ruby*'s home*

TIME
The present

PEARL: Ruby…Honey…I won't have you talk like this. I don't mean to sound unsympathetic, but it's utter nonsense. Listen…you're a fantastic person. You've got a good head on your shoulders and lots of guts—after all, you're the one who took the initiative to get out of this dying marriage, didn't you? And you have the same spirit and ambition that drives your father and me. You're going to go out there and be great. You've already been through the tough times—they're over now. The good times are just beginning. Starting with tomorrow.

Tomorrow, you'll go into your lawyer's office with your head held high and proud and everyone in the room will become unnerved.

Why? Because everyone will expect you to be weepy and emotional, but you'll throw them all for a loop by being in control. You'll wrap up this chapter of your life with a grand finale. Remember my last night? I was back at Radio City Music Hall for the 50th Anniversary show. What a reunion! I was with all the old girls again, and we had a great time rehearsing and reminiscing. So, there we were on opening night with all these famous people in the audience. Well, you know old Pearl and her damn vanity! I was getting ready to go out on stage and I realized I'm wearing my glasses. Well, there's no way I was going to make my big return to show biz in those ugly bifocals with the blue plastic frames! So, I took them off and tossed them in the dressing room. And look what happened! The orchestra began playing and I came out on stage with the girls, dancing and smiling brightly. We did some high kicks together and then unlocked our arms, and suddenly, I was so overwhelmed by the cheers of the audience, that I lost my bearings, missed a step, and went tumbling into the orchestra pit! I fell right into the woodwinds and got a piccolo up my ass!

Is seems awful, but Honey—what a way to go! I died right in the midst of doing the one thing in my life that made me happy and fulfilled. And such an exit! I died with a bang—not with a whimper. I was all over the eleven o'clock news and on the front page of the New York *Post*! I had a grand funeral with dozens of famous people in attendance. The Cardinal came from St. Patrick's Cathedral—and I'm not even Catholic!

I finished triumphantly, with my pride in full force, even though it was my pride that led to my demise. And they say, "Pride goeth before a fall." Bull! So, that's what I want you to do. Go out and end it on a good note. I did! I think it was B flat, actually.

SILENCE
BY BRIAN DYKSTRA

ALASKA *is an "at risk" kid in a summer arts program.* SHE *has been up all night, drinking cheap sweet wine, after another kid killed himself the day before.* SHE *talks to her only friend in the program.*

SCENE
Outside the rehearsal studio

TIME
Just after dawn

ALASKA: He was really very charming. Asked me out. Figured, by now, word gets out pretty quick, and he just wanted to get something easy. But, who was I, right? Figured, what the hell, I went out with him. He walked me to my door. That night. First date. Put his hand on my shoulder, told me he had a real good time, and he left. Figured he was being nice. Didn't really have a good time. I was too whatever, for him. But he stopped on the way to his car and repeated it. Had a real good time and could we get together again? I said, sure (like I could take it or leave it) and he took off... Called the next day. That was quick. Wanted to see me. We went out, again. Same thing. Dropped me off. No fooling around. Nothing like that. Go out a few more times, and we find ourselves alone in a place, we're drinking. I figure, here it comes. We're alone, alcohol, he's going to make a move. And he does. And I'm cool with it. I remember wishing I had more booze in me, but he was pretty cute. Anyway, he stops himself. Gets all apologetic, stuff about drinking. I think he's covering his ass, or something, but I hear him say some stuff about wanting to do this sober. Like that's important for some reason. He looks in my eyes, and says some really nice things, and it hits me that he really wants me. Really. He's stopping himself. Pulls away, kind of shaking, takes me home. Like he's mad at himself for losing control. He says some more really nice things. I can't figure it out, because basically that thought never occurred to me, before. But, this guy likes me. But really, he really likes me. Not because I put out. Not because I'm some stoned party girl who will do anything. This guy actually likes me ... me ... for me. I mean, I been with sixty-six people, and had yet to find one who I thought liked me.

So, next time we get together, I practically rape him. I mean, I couldn't get enough of this guy. And he was so into me. I got all panicked when I didn't see him, that somebody would tell him how much of a slut I was. Every time he came back, it was panic until he smiled and looked at me with those eyes, and we ended up in bed, again.

...Took me awhile. I start to notice we only get together to have sex. I mean, it was a lot, and it was great, but we never went out. Never. Thought maybe someone told him, and he was ashamed being seen with me. So I gather my courage up, and ask him. And he said, no, that had not happened. It was the way he said that. And the way he took the question. Because, by asking, I was basically telling him what a slut I was. But he just said what he said, "No, that had not happened." And it was like he was waiting for something: When it hit me. I looked at the guy and I said, "You knew the whole time, didn't you?" And he smiled like a ... like a camp counselor who was proud of something one of the campers finally figured out on their own. He smiled, breathed a sigh … He actually patted me somewhere. I was too numb to remember if it was my elbow, or arm, or shoulder, or even a pat on the back, but he patted me somewhere and said, "I was starting to worry. Thank God you finally figured that out." See, he wasn't going to be in town long. But he wasn't just looking for a fuck. Not this guy. He was looking for a great fuck. And I fucked him like I loved him. No, that's not true, better than that. I fucked him like he loved me. Things I never thought I'd ever do. For longer than I thought I could do them. So, I thought I knew some stuff. Been around. Didn't figure there was much more I had to find out. But then you meet someone so out of your league, it just makes you step back. That there are people so much colder out there. You know the scariest thing? The way he said it. Like I said, from a camp counselor. Like, because of who I was, it was okay for him to do that. That's not it, exactly. It was more like he was teaching me a lesson. Not in a bad way, but teaching me something I needed to know. For later. Like he saw it in me, what he was. And I could take what he taught me, and get better sex off some boy in the future. Like, we were in this secret club, now. Him and me, and whoever else he did that to, and whoever I ever did it to. So, anyway, he was number sixty-seven.

THE SIX THAT FELL

BY LAURA HENRY

Six women meet regularly to compare their efforts in conceiving a child. SMALL CAPS:ERMINE*'s experience is unusual.*

SCENE
A street corner

TIME
The present

ERMINE: It's not my fault that we can't have children. Rick has Kleinfelter's Syndrome. I think it's all in his mind, but he swears he can't control it. Men. So we've got to get somebody else's sperm. It really pissed me off. I know it shouldn't, but it does. I married Rick for several reasons: 1) he's smart, 2) he's got great ancestry and 3) he's incredibly attractive. Perfect breeding material. Except, of course, for the Kleinfelter's thing. But I didn't know about that when I married him. And I did say that I would marry him for better or for worse. If I had to do it over again, I would probably write my own vows. But I didn't. And it's too late now.

I've pored over all these books of men, looking for the perfect stud sperm. The cute ones can't spell. The ones who can spell are all short. It's incredibly frustrating. I've taken to the streets, looking for a perfect man: tall with brown hair and blue eyes, a little gangly, a sexy smile, a good grasp of the English language. A man just like Rick who has better sperm. This drives my mother nuts. "So what are you going to do," she wants to know, "Just run up to some stranger and ask him for his SPERM?" Precisely, I tell her. People are more giving than we typically expect them to be. I'm sure lots of men would be willing to donate. We, as women, are just not nervy enough to ask.

So one night I found him. My perfect donor. I was on the southeast corner of Mockingbird and Irvine, he was standing southwest. Dark shrouded the city like a widow's mourning veil. Slowly, my eyes began to adjust to the dark, and a silhouette in the distance began to sharpen. Gangly, sexy, tall … Could it be? I couldn't tell. I sauntered over to him. The lack of light heightened the sense in my fingertips, and as I shook his hand, the familiar sensation sent chills up my spine. Warm, safe, and oh so right. Rick, this man, they could have been brothers. It was a risk, but a risk I knew I had to take.

I've been looking for you all my life, I said.

He smiled. He ran his finger across the nape of my neck. It tingled.

I had found my man. Can I take you home, he asked? Yes, yes, yes, yes, yes. How lucky could I get? No artificial insemination, no huge doctor bills, no long waiting period. This was it.

He had this blindfold. He blindfolded me. It was so sexy. He put me in his car, drove me to this mysterious place, walked me up the front path and pushed me through the front door. I was so turned on I just wanted to scream. He took off the blindfold—I blinked in the light. And then I realized I was standing right in the middle of my own living room. The guy that looked like Rick WAS Rick. It figures. Great sex, no cigar.

SMALL DOMESTIC ACTS

BY JOAN LIPKIN

Two working-class couples, a heterosexual couple, and a lesbian couple become friends. As problems become apparent in the relationships, the possibility of a new couple emerges, thus calling into question gender roles, the potential fluidity of sexuality and identity and the definition of family. In this speech, Straight Sheila *discusses the early pressure she felt to pursue a heterosexual relationship without exploring or even questioning her own desire or other options.*

SCENE
A stage

TIME
The present

(She *comes downstage center and addresses the audience. We are now back in the present.* She *tells the story of their courtship as if it is the first time* She *has ever said it aloud.* She *is alternately embarrassed, defiant, explanatory, distressed, and confused, and only realizes the significance of what* She *is saying as* She *comes towards the end of her speech. It is a mutual discovery for both her and the audience.*)

Straight Sheila: The sex was the easy part. Once you get past doing it the first time. Well, the first *few* times. The first time I slept with Frank, I was scared to death. Scared he wouldn't like what he saw.

I'd be too ripe. My breasts would jiggle. Turns out that's what he likes. But I didn't know that at the time. I wanted to say, wait. But I was scared I'd lose him. He'd find some other girl that would and he wouldn't even know the difference. (*Beat.*) I was okay on my own. I had a job and a regular bank account. It wasn't much, what with the rent and the utilities and my car payment. It was the first time I had something that was all mine. But damn if my friends didn't make me feel like I was doing something all wrong. There we'd be, having a pizza, or a few drinks, and it would be men. And if they weren't talking about men, they'd be working real hard *not* to talk about them. Laughing too loud, tossing their hair back at the bar. I figured the only way to get away from this man thing...was to get one. So when I met Frank and liked him okay, I thought this is it. You've got to make a decision sometimes. So this thing with Frank happened pretty quickly. Before I know it, we're living together. One day, I wake up and say, who is this man I sleep next to every night? Who is he really? Who am I? (*Beat.*) When I think back on how nervous I was. Would he like me? And would it be okay in bed? Shoot, that's the easy part. Talking and getting along day to day is what's hard. All I could think about was would he like me. I was so busy thinking about would he like me, I never stopped to think...did I like him?

SOME GIRL(s)

BY NEIL LABUTE

The reunion of Guy *and* Sam *after fifteen years has begun awkwardly.* He *is on the verge of marriage and has wanted to visit old girlfriends to see whether* He *has missed the "perfect one."* She *reminds him that* He *broke off the relationship and says that* She *heard that* He *took a girl to the senior prom at another high school.*

SCENE
A fairly standard hotel room

TIME
The present

Sam: I overheard it once, just a mention of it one time in the store … you know, where you almost ended up. In your *vision*. I was in there, dropping off lunch for my husband and I was looking at something. I don't remember what now, some new thing on an end cap display — *cookies* or whatever — and I hear a voice, a woman's voice that I recognize, this blast from the past. It's your mother. Your mom, standing in the juice aisle and talking to somebody, a neighbor lady or from church, and they're going on about the good ol' days, like women do, and somehow they get on the subject of proms. Of big dances. Maybe because her daughter — not your mom obviously, but the other woman — her last kid is getting ready for hers, and off they go, chatting about this and that. I don't mean to … but I keep standing there and listening and, boy, do I get an earful! About you, and us, and, well, lots. Lots of *stuff*. And part of that "stuff" is how nice you look — how well you "cleaned up," she called it — for your big night. *Prom* night. And imagine me, standing there next to this Hearty Fudge Crunch, and I'm thinking, "What night? I didn't have a big night. We didn't go to any prom." But of course she wasn't talking about me. Or us. No, this was about you. The night she was referring to was all about *you*. And her … some girl. (*Beat.*) She also said you don't call home enough. Your mom did.

SONGS OF THE DRAGONS FLYING TO HEAVEN

BY YOUNG JEAN LEE

A cute, 20-something Asian-American female stands center stage. SHE *is wearing jeans, black-and-white checkered Vans, and a pink shirt with a giraffe on it.*

SCENE
Anywhere, U.S.A.

TIME
The present

KOREAN-AMERICAN: Have you ever noticed how most Asian-Americans are slightly brain-damaged from having grown up with Asian parents?

It's like being raised by monkeys— these retarded monkeys who can barely speak English and are too evil to understand anything besides conformity and status. Most of us hate these monkeys from an early age and try to learn how to be human from school or television, but the result is always tainted by this subtle or not-so-subtle retardation. Asian people from Asia are even more brain-damaged, but in a different way, because they are the original monkey. Anyway, some white men who like Asian women seem to like this retarded quality as well, and sometimes the more retarded the better.

I am so mad about all of the racist things against me in this country, which is America.

Like the fact that the reason why so many white men date Asian women is that they can get better-looking Asian women than they can get white women because we are easier to get and have lower self-esteem. It's like going with an inferior brand so that you can afford more luxury features. Also, Asian women will date white guys who no white woman would touch.

But the important thing about being Korean is getting to know your roots. Because we come to this country and want to forget about our ancestry, but this is bad, and we have to remember that our grandfathers and grandmothers were people too, with interesting stories to tell.

Which leads to a story from my grandmother, which is the story of the mudfish.

In Korea they have this weird thing where everyone turns a year older on New Year's day. So if you were born on December 31, you turn one on January 1st even though you've only been alive for a day. Anyway, each year on New Year's day, my grandmother used to make this special dish called meekudaji tang that she would only serve once a year because it was such a pain in the ass to make.

The main ingredient of meekudaji tang is mudfish, which are these tiny fishes they have in Korea that live on muddy riverbanks and eat mud. Every New Year's day, my grandmother would throw a bunch of mudfish into a bowl of brine, which would make them puke out all their mud until they were shiny clean. Then she would put pieces of tofu on a skillet, heat it up, and throw the live mudfish onto the skillet. The mudfish would frantically burrow inside the pieces of tofu to escape the heat and, voilà, stuffed tofu!

White people are so alert to any infringement on their rights. It's really funny. And the reason why it's funny is that minorities have all the power. We can take the word racism and hurl it at people and demolish them and there's nothing you can do to stop us.

I feel so much pity for you right now.

You have no idea what's going on. The wiliness of the Korean is beyond anything that you could ever hope to imagine.

I can promise you one thing, which is that we will crush you. You may laugh now, but remember my words when you and your offspring are writhing under our yoke.

(*Pause. Raising her fist.*)

Let the Korean dancing begin!

SOUL HEALING

BY BOB SHUMAN

REVEREND ELIZABETH, *a Spiritualist minister, is in her late 30s; she wears a dark blue suit with a clerical collar. After church meetings, SISTER CATHERINE, a Catholic nun, greets her.*

SCENE
A hotel conference room in southeastern Pennsylvania

TIME
Tonight

REVEREND ELIZABETH: Sister Catherine? How are you doing? If I had known you were going to be here, I would have taken part in the study group. They're using the old convent reading lists, talking about St. Teresa and Padre Pio. I'm just sorry I'm on my way out. I have an early morning, giving a fundraising speech. What has it been? Eight, nine years, at least. (*Pause.*)

It gets stuffy in here without the air conditioning. Please take off your coat. I can stay a few minutes. You've lost weight, I have to say—sit down—I hope not too much. (*Pause.*)

Paul usually gives the demonstrations, but he's in England training: physical phenomena, clairvoyance. Come back one Sunday and you can hear me preach. (*Writing a note.*) I'm going to give you the name of a healer—I can only imagine what you think of this. You should take it, please let me give it to you—[(Sister Catherine *refuses the note concerning the healer.*)] I said a voice told me to go in the convent. (Reverend Elizabeth *takes back the note.*) Sending me to volunteer at rehab, it took me a while to realize you were trying to punish me.

I have to finish my speech before it gets too late. (*Silence.*)

(Reverend Elizabeth *looks through her papers.*) Sister Clare's mother, after she passed away, there was another voice . . . "Won't you offer my daughter my apologies? Would she forgive me?" She woke me up in the middle of the night. Broke into my meditations and prayers. I lit votives and went twice a day to Mass, "Tell my daughter I ask for her love . . ."

(*Silence.*)

(*Practicing her speech.*) "It's easier to pick up a brick and put it in the ground than it is to stop abuse. (*Making notes.*) It's easier to have the miraculous communicated in the pages of a book than through a medium such as myself. We're building this church together because it's easier to put a brick down than it is to live one more second in hating yourself—"

The night manager is signalling to me, he wants to lock up.

I'm sorry, Sister Catherine. If you're not going to let me help you . . . it's not something I need to be tested on. All you thought was I was upsetting the novices with hallucinations, probably schizophrenic . . .

(*Pause.*)

(*Calling out to the night manager.*) Jimmy, I'm with someone I know. You don't mind if we stay a while longer. You can start turning off the lights if you want—we don't care.

(*The lights are lowered.*)

(*To* SISTER CATHERINE.) I guess I should be humbled you're even here. I know why you came, it's not for my personality. God called me to enter the convent. I wanted to save the world, found out I couldn't do that. I could save myself, maybe. I took the holy vows; I broke them, not because of you ... not because of you, Sister Catherine, who wanted to get me out ... but because I couldn't stay any longer and honor *myself*, who I was! I did hear voices, I did see—I won't let you or anyone tell me I didn't—I took the ring off. *I* left Him.

(*Pause.*)

(*Calling out, suddenly, to the spirit world.*) Let's get going! I've got two people here who need to go to work in the morning.

(*Silence.*)

Sometimes I think of Sister Frances crying "Mama" before the death rattle. The old nuns asking me to read Hildegard of Bingen, "I, the fiery life of divine wisdom, I ignite the beauty of the plains, I sparkle the waters, I burn in the beauty of the sun, and the moon, and the stars." (*Silence. Scanning her speech.*)

I'll look at this again tomorrow, I'm too tired now. "To believe that there must be somebody else out there just like you, it must be easier than to imagine you're alone." (*Pause.*) You won't mind if I leave when I'm through packing up. I understand you don't want to talk—I don't mean to be mad. (*Another set of lights is turned off.*)

(*Silence.*)

(Reverend Elizabeth *senses a spirit.*) A young man…You know who he is, he's saying. He shows me the image of a crow, like one you saw this morning. I'm aware of St. Anne, the church where his urn is buried: Thomas. He assures me he didn't take drugs like crack and cocaine. It started with pills only to get high. He's your sister's son, does any of this make sense to you? His roommate never noticed or thought he was being forgetful, planning a retreat. Thomas takes the medication, slowly, not to be caught: Xanex, Tylenol with codeine, Halcyon, OxyContin, a precious capsule of morphine—anything, anything he can get his hands on. Carefully he builds his stock, only to be told someone would be checking up on him, staying part of the time, watching—you.

(*Gaining intensity as the lights fade.*) He doesn't want you to be hurt. He's sorry for any trouble he's caused you. He couldn't face his depression, he's saying. He knows you didn't know how to help him. You can't stop it, no matter what you do. You can't wake him up. You can't lift his body any further. Come back to life. You're the one who's alone. You're the one who's dead! (*Silence.*) I won't leave you.

SOUVENIR
BY STEPHEN TEMPERLEY

FLORENCE FOSTER JENKINS *is a wealthy society woman who, though she believes herself to be a great soprano, has no voice and is incapable of singing two notes in tune. Her belief in her talent, however, and her dedication to music and the art of singing are absolute. She behaves at all times as if she is a major vocal artist. There must be no hint of mockery. She interviews a possible accompanist, Mr. McMoon.*

SCENE
An elegant room at the Ritz-Carlton

TIME
1932

FLORENCE FOSTER JENKINS: What matters most is the music you hear in your head. Don't you agree, Mr. McMoon? The impossible ideal, as it were. The beauty not *quite* within our grasp. I have always had a great love of music. It's the music that draws me. It's the music that must come before all else. (*Sits on the bench.*) Let me be frank. While singing for friends I have allowed myself to be accompanied by those who could not always give the music its due. Without wishing to give offense, for this my first *public* recital I must be (*Gently.*) ruthless. I seek no reward for my singing—certainly no financial reward—no personal *réclame*, I assure you. But this is no mere act of vanity.

[**Mr. McMoon:** Mrs. Foster Jen…]

Florence Foster Jenkins: (*Rises. Crosses towards him. Politely.*) Please…let me finish. I know how it might seem: a woman like myself comes to a man like you—from out of nowhere—declaring herself ready to scale the pinnacles of the soprano repertoire. You could think me no more than a mere *dilettante…*

[**Mr. McMoon:** Mrs. Foster Jen…]

Florence Foster Jenkins: (*More politely.*) … no, please let me finish! I've sung many times for charity. In various drawing rooms. Friends have been kind enough to compliment me on the depth of my feeling. Which is why it has now been *proposed* that my name on a handbill might prove an attraction. Among my own circle, you understand. I don't speak of the public at large. But still, enough to fill a modest hall. Which is rather exciting, don't you think? What I seek—have sought, am seeking—is a colleague, a collaborator, a soul mate.

[**Mr. McMoon:** Mrs. Fost…]

Florence Foster Jenkins: (*Even more politely.*) No, please, you *must* let me finish! Let me say at once that I would not expect you to undertake such a task without a remuneration that I intend to be fully commensurate with your dignity. Now. What do you say?

[**Mr. McMoon:** (*Cautious.*) It's by no means impossible…what you ask.]

Florence Foster Jenkins: (*Grateful.*) I thank you for that. You have given me hope.

[**Mr. McMoon:** It's a matter of polishing, you say—?]

FLORENCE FOSTER JENKINS: And perfecting. Refining. May I confide in you, Mr. McMoon? You won't think me foolish? Some weeks ago I dreamed I was singing in public.

[**MR. McMOON:** Yes?]

FLORENCE FOSTER JENKINS: Do you know what it was that I sang? In my dream? The famous aria of the Queen of the Night (*Reverent.*) *Der Hölle Rache kocht in meinem Herzem! Tod und Verzweiflung flammen um mich her!* The very words produce chills.

(SHE *shudders. Utters a small shriek.* [McMOON *is at a loss for words.*)

You are familiar with that particular aria?

MR. McMOON: *Zauberflöte.*

FLORENCE FOSTER JENKINS: *Comment?*

MR. McMOON: Magic Flute

FLORENCE FOSTER JENKINS: Exactly!] And who do you think was in the audience, smiling up at me, encouraging me? Mr. Mozart.

[**MR. McMOON:** Mr…?]

FLORENCE FOSTER JENKINS: Mozart! I would hardly call myself a follower of Mr. Freud but the meaning seemed all too apparent. Did I have it in my voice, I wondered? Few sopranos are equipped to tackle the Queen of the Night. As you're no doubt aware, the aria's range is extensive. I had my doubts. One is only human after all. (*Laughs. Stops herself abruptly.*) However—and this is almost too uncanny—the next day—the very next day, Mr.

McMoon! —while riding in a taxicab on Lexington, I found myself in a slight collision. The *f* above *c* burst from me spontaneously.

[**MR. McMOON:** (*Bewildered.*) The *f* above *c?*]

FLORENCE FOSTER JENKINS: Passersby were enraptured, amazed. I stepped from the wreckage a new woman. But enough talk. Let's take the plunge. Shall we make music? Shall we see how we suit? (*Inviting him to sit at the piano.*) S'il vous plaît?

(SHE *crosses to a cabinet from which she brings a sheaf of music returning with it to the piano.*)

FLORENCE FOSTER JENKINS: (*Turning over sheet music for individual arias.*) *La Fanciula?* Perhaps not before lunch. *Così?* So grateful to the voice. *Lucia?* She presents a fascinating problem does she not? How to sing in Italian while at the same time suggesting a Scottish burr. Please. Should I mention some special favorite—shout it out! (*Scanning the contents of an album.*) *Bohème, Faust, Rosenkavalier.* Each delicious in its way. Ah! Dear *Rigoletto*! *Caro nome?* Perfect. You are acquainted, I assume, with the work of Mr. Verdi? Modern music isn't to everyone's taste, I know.

(SHE *settles Caro Nome on the piano then hurries back to the curve, readying herself to sing.*)

Mr. McMoon? Á vôtre plaisir.

SPINE

BY JESSIE MCCORMACK

JULIE, *early-to-mid-20s, has told friends she is at a "Spa," but it's actually a posh therapeutic retreat.* SHE *is talking to her therapist.*

SCENE
Therapist's office

TIME
The present

JULIE: …So I was eight years old and my father started giving me an allowance. Twenty bucks a week. Even at the time I remember thinking, "Why is Dad giving me so much money? It's not appropriate for a child my age." And then on top of that he always made me carry an extra fifty dollar bill around. That was "mug money."

See, homeless men would often prey upon little kids walking home from private school so in the event that I ever got mugged, my father wanted to make sure I always had enough cash on me. That way my attacker wouldn't get mad and seek retribution somehow.

So every morning before school my father would yell from the den: "Don't spend your 'mug money.'" And this eventually took its toll on me. I started walking around in complete fear that I was gonna get mugged all the time—in the playground, during 'snack time,' wherever I was, and then I started fixating on the idea that fifty dollars wasn't enough money to satisfy a person who went to all the trouble of attacking me so then I started saving up my allowance and using it as supplemental 'mug money' until I wound up walking around with like six hundred dollars on my person.

And then one day it happened. I was walking down Riverside Drive and this man came up to me and demanded I give him all my money. And he became completely shocked when he saw how much I had on me. He kept asking what a kid my age was doing, carrying around that much cash. And then he started making fun of my wallet. It was one of those tiny, plastic "Hello Kitty" wallets with the velcro flap, and he kept saying if I was gonna carry so many bills then I oughtta get a big leather wallet, a real '*man*'s wallet,' not this flimsy, little, 'pussy' wallet I was using. And I didn't know what he meant by that so I said, "It's not a 'Little Pussy' wallet, it's a 'Hello Kitty' wallet." And he laughed. I made my assailant laugh. I remember taking some sort of strange pride in that even though I didn't understand what he was laughing about.

Then he said if I told anyone about this he would come find me. And that was it. I looked away and he was gone. I did eventually tell my father and all he did was berate me for walking down Riverside Drive. "Always take West End, there are more door men around." After that I wasn't so afraid of getting mugged anymore. The fear just kinda disappeared. I did get a new wallet, though.

SPINE
BY JESSIE MCCORMACK

GWYNN, *early-to-mid-20s, has told friends she is at a "Spa," but it's actually a posh therapeutic retreat.* SHE *is talking to her therapist.*

SCENE
Therapist's office

TIME
The present

GWYNN: I have no skills. None. I don't know how to do…anything. All I do is take up space. Ask me if I can do something and I bet you I can't. I don't know how to type. I don't know how to do laundry. I don't know how to drive stick-shift. I don't know how to pump gas. It's disgusting. I'm like a…I'm like a…I'm like a half-person.

I don't understand how people deal with the minutiae of everyday life. Like bills. People actually pay their bills on time. Every single month. And they remember to take their clothing to the dry cleaners and then they remember to pick up their clothing from the dry cleaners and I just, I can't keep track of it all; it's too overwhelming and I've seriously thought about moving into a retirement community 'cos all of that stuff's taken care of for you but I can't do that now because this…this man came along and…and…and…and…he's willing to put up with all of my…ya know, with me, he's willing to put up with me which is INSANE and that makes him a little insane, right? I mean, doesn't it?

And now he wants to open a school with me, a scuba diving school, ya know, to teach people how to…how to scuba dive, obviously. But I don't know anything about how to run a scuba diving school! And his response is, "Well, neither do I …. we'll learn together." And then I start thinking, okay, maybe we could learn together, that sounds like fun and then that gets me thinking like, huh, maybe it's not too late for me; maybe there's still time for me to make something out of my godforsaken waste of a life but then I think, no, no, no, I'm relying on a man to make me feel better, I can't do that but then I think why the hell not? I mean, that's why people couple up because they make each other feel better, until they don't anymore and then I get all sad because what if that day comes, the day when he stops making me feel better. Then I'll be right back where I started. Only now I have no skills and I have a broken heart. I'll be a broken-hearted, skill-less, space-taker.

But then I always go back to the two of us taking a dive together…and I can't seem to shake that from my mind. Just the idea of spending my days under the sea with the man I love…I dunno. That seems like a nice way of life.

Sometimes I wish I were a mermaid. But we should probably save that for another session, right?

STRING FEVER

BY JACQUELYN REINGOLD

A music teacher, Lily, *just turned 40, still mourns her breakup with an unstable musician, with whom she had hoped to marry and start a family. She is on a date with a physicist, the father of one of her students, as she contemplates a future filled with limited options.*

SCENE
An Italian restaurant

TIME
The present

Lily: I have nothing to complain about. I have so much. I get to start over. I get to, uh, date. Like now, like here. I'm having a goddamn date. I haven't had a date since, well, ever maybe. But I met you, and look: you're smart, you're good looking, we're eating, we're on a date. So no complaints. I'm healthy. I can be a parent. Like you. Even if it's on my own. Right? Even if it's on my own. And even if I adopt. Even if I never have another date, and I have to stop playing the violin 'cause I can't afford it. So I'm not—so I don't make records, and things didn't turn out the way I. Isn't that what being mature is? Acceptance. Gratitude. At a certain point. Everything isn't possible anymore. Isn't that right? It's just that. Maybe a lobotomy. You know? Maybe a goddamn selective lobotomy! That would help.

TEOTWAWKI
BY JO J. ADAMSON

A power outage at the casino results in three middle-aged women exchanging personal information. HANNAH, *a cigarette dangling from her lips, reveals her former involvement with a feminist group and how she became a slots player.*

SCENE
A casino

TIME
The present

HANNAH: I never tried to torch my bra, but I once joined a feminist group. The book discussion group was full and I was feeling a little uneasy with my life and so I thought I'd give it a go.

My husband asked why I wanted to join a group of hysterical females. Well, there wasn't a "hysterical" female in the lot. But there were plenty of angry females, and frustrated females, and females who wore no makeup or bras. These women wanted something more than marriage, kids, and a mortgage. They wanted to "find themselves." I made fun of them. "Find yourselves? Why, are you lost?" I become sarcastic when I'm uneasy. And these women made me very uneasy. One woman suggested that they might threaten me. "Threaten me? Don't be absurd," I said. "I'm a happily married woman with a full life."

"If that's true, why are you here?"

I like to read, I said lamely. The truth of the matter was I didn't know why I was there. There was a big empty hole around my heart, and I wanted to fill it up. I was becoming invisible, and I wanted people to see me.

When I tried to tell Henry what transpired in the sessions, it sounded so silly. Phrases like "my own space," "my own body" tripped off my tongue until I felt like the walking feminist bible, *Our Bodies, Ourselves.*

I misquoted Gloria Steinem and Germaine Greer. I told Henry he was as worthless as a fish on a bicycle. That I'd dwindled into a wife, and if men had to have abortions, it would become a sacrament.

I spewed out all the rhetoric of the women's movement as if it were divine law and before long I had stopped wearing a bra and I'd let my hair go back to its natural color. Gray.

Henry was beside himself. What did I want? A divorce? A Hawaiian vacation? A trip to Las Vegas, what?

I wasn't "fulfilled," I said. That was the other "F" word in the '80s.

Henry finally gave me an ultimatum—choose that militant women's group or him. I couldn't have both.

My last meeting was on a Halloween night. We were having a little party and I came as a Humpty Dumpty. It somehow fit.

"Trick or Treat," I said after we downed a bottle of Merlot. "I'm outa here."

What have we done? Are we too extreme? Many of them were divorced or had alternative life styles.

(HANNAH *looks at Bertha.*)

That means they have sleepovers with their girlfriends, Bertha.

[BERTHA: I know what a lesbian is. I watched "Ellen" come out on national TV!]

Why was I leaving the group, they demanded. I had learned a lot and had opened myself up to them. I thought long and hard about it, and then it hit me.

I was leaving because if I stayed I would have to admit that my entire life—my marriage, my children, and my friendships was one big lie. If those women knew what they were talking about, my life would be invalid. Unjustifiable, and irrelevant: it would have no more meaning than an expired driver's license.

"I am forty-five years old. Too old to want my own space." Shoot, I didn't even know we *had* our own space. Mine was always full of *people*.

I left the group and like Humpty Dumpty remained sitting on the wall. I wasn't happy and I wasn't unhappy. I was just present and accounted for.

When Henry retired, we found out that we didn't have much in common. We didn't have much to say to one another. Hell, I'm not even sure we even *like* one another.

He does his thing, golf, and I do mine, play games, and never the twain should meet. I hate golf and he wouldn't be caught dead inside of a casino.

It works for us.

TRAIN STORY
BY ADAM RAPP

On her way to a weekend rendezvous by train to L.A. from New York, a WOMAN *recounts her encounter with a belligerent teenaged passenger,* EXLEY, *who turns out to be dying from a botched abortion.*

SCENE
A stage in a cone of light

TIME
The present

WOMAN: Well, wherever you wind up I wish you luck, Exley.

> She doesn't respond. It's as if I've stung her. Sure, an overly educated, more fortunate white woman in designer clothes can just throw Luck around. It's a mild luxury like potpourri or expensive soap.

> When the conductor re-enters I tell him how Exley may be hemorrhaging from her uterus and he calls the paramedics on his walkie-talkie. She is staring out the window as if there is something in the barren fields that will pardon her. As if there is a fairy tale about poor white girls that has yet to be written.

> We lock eyes for a moment. Bravely. Somehow longingly. I never used to believe that strangers shared these kind of moments.

Those café scenes in French films. The intimate camera angle. The chamber music. It all adds so much. Even in novels. The description of the fading light. The moon hidden in the prose. In real life these exchanges are simply anecdotes. Little stories that turn into a kind of conversational currency. A four-minute curiosity to be tweaked and shaped. But nothing more. It's never about yearning or frailty or pure, wordless human contact.

By the time the train stops in Indiana Exley has lost consciousness. There is an enormous volume of blood pooling in her lap. When the doors open there are policemen. There are station managers. There are paramedics as silent as aliens. Far too many men to move the body of a small, lifeless girl.

I tell one of the paramedics that I think it's a botched abortion. I give him the number where I'm staying and ask him to call me. To let me know if she makes it through.

That evening I move my things into the café car and eat the tasteless food and continue line editing my young author's clumsy first novel. I sleep restlessly in a clenched seated position.

Two days later I arrive on the West Coast and my publishing friend picks me up in a Range Rover. Howard Slutes has shaved his moustache and I don't like it. I don't like his hands or his mouth or those little bumps on his neck, either. But despite my misgivings we feign mutual romantic interest and drink a bottle of wine and perform clinical sexual intercourse in the froth of the Pacific Ocean. Out of loneliness more than anything else. Why I have to travel across the country to make love to a man I barely know I have no idea. Is it ambition? Or ego? Or the need to collect a story? Maybe it's some kind of absurd attempt at preservation of the species? Plain old-fashioned animal fucking. An ape fuck. Perhaps it's the simple need to get away from myself? That's what happens when we cloister off in the city. The years add up like so many forgotten fruit rinds and we're left with the unpleasant mystery of our own sour-smelling skin.

His body is like salty beef. I notice more horrible imperfections. Moles and scars and pockets of flab. He tells me that he has had a vasectomy. His cock is hard and small and when he comes he sounds like a woman. He toots like a clarinet.

We spend the next few days together talking about Graham Greene and the new fall list, which features three of my authors. We continue fucking with a forced inevitability that somehow makes me think of pontoon boats.

A few weeks after I get back to New York I start to feel sick in the mornings. I think I must have gotten a bug from traveling. Something from the other coast. That inexplicable way time zones corrupt the immune system. All that trapped train air.

Three weeks later I miss my period. I am vomiting like a frat boy. I buy an over-the-counter pregnancy test. It turns out positive.

I am two months along now. My breasts have swollen. My appetite has changed. I have told no one. Not even Howard Slutes and his purported vasectomy. When he calls me at work we talk about Graham Greene and the prep school novel. He'll sell it well, he says. The buyers in his region are excited.

I often think of Exley. That paramedic never called me. I don't recall what she did or said so much as her will. How it burned through her skin. That lost white orchid. Did she make it through? Did someone find her at the hospital? A priest? A policeman? A man with a guitar? Is she wandering the snow-swept highways of Indiana?

There are certain hours of the night when I wake to the sound of a train. It roars right through my apartment. At times it feels as if it will lift me out of bed. All that earsplitting thunder and then silence. A quiet that can't be captured in prose or likened to certain kinds of weather. A calm that defies even thought. Just the purest absence of noise.

Perhaps souls have the ability to leap from womb to womb? Like invisible tree frogs.

I am alone, Exley. I am very much alone in a city that at times makes people feel old and used. But I am somehow lucky. Even during the darkest hour I manage to always pull through…

THE 29 QUESTIONS PROJECT

BY HILLARY ROLLINS

ACTRESS 1 *addresses the 29 questions, originally a light-hearted Internet game played with her close friend* LAURA. *Now all that remains of her friend, post 9/11, is in her "voice." As* ACTRESS 1 *reiterates answers to the questions a final time, some have changed utterly, and others have taken on new meaning due to her loss and grief.*

SCENE
A New York apartment

TIME
October 2001

ACTRESS 1: It's like she simply evaporated. Except for these twenty-nine questions stored on my hard drive. (ACTRESS 1 *reads or types a new version of the questionnaire.*) 1: Living arrangement—I live with it, like we all do. And I also live with my sensitive, anxious, needy two-year-old for whom I must be dependable, ever-steady Mommy—protector, source, authority, haven,— "Mommy happy?" she asks me in a tiny, pathetic voice. "Mommy no sad?" Preternaturally brilliant as she *is*, of course, she couldn't have understood what happened. Yet in the days following the attacks she began demanding that we turn off the television when the news was on—"No like it! No like it!"—and started mumbling things like, "I'm safe. I'm safe with Mommy, I'm safe with Daddy…" So part of my new "living arrangement" is to go outside to the car to cry. 2: What book are you reading now? Forget it. When the cute little dictator doesn't force me to turn it off, I'm glued to the TV news like everybody else. (Who was it who said when the revolution comes it will not be televised?) 3: What's on your mouse pad? No mouse pad — I have a touch pad on a laptop and I continue to try and write. 4: Future child's name? Laura. 5: Chocolate or vanilla? Both! And as often as possible. Maybe I'll just never diet again, you know? And while we're at it, 6a: Favorite smells? All of them, everything my greedy little nostrils can inhale, I can't get enough. 6b: Least favorite smell? Rotting flesh. 7: Favorite sound? Children laughing is good, so is the sound of my daughter sleeping soundly. Also, fabulous music. Laura had a strikingly beautiful singing voice. We sang together a lot — Sondheim and Gershwin, (and Rodgers and Hart,) James Taylor and Laura Nero, and she knew a terrific harmony to "Amazing Grace." [8: Least favorite sound? "Amazing Grace" played on the bagpipes. 9.] What is the first thing you think of when you wake up in the morning? Usually I try to remember to be grateful for the day and what's ahead. (10: If you could have any job you wanted what would it be? Flag salesman. 11.) How many rings before you answer the phone? … You know, a few days later I called her house — I don't know why. Of course the machine picked up with Laura's voice on it. I don't know what I was thinking. It was a stupid thing to do. (12. Do you like to drive fast? *No*. 13: What is your favorite number? Two thousand nine hundred and thirty-six. Or one. 14:) Favorite alcoholic drink? A half-empty half-full glass of good red wine and I wouldn't mind one right about now. 15: What's under your bed? Boogeymen. 16, 17, 18, 19: Say one nice thing about the person who sent this to you. If you could meet one person dead or alive? Worst feeling in the world? What is the most important thing in life?

(*Pause.*)

ACTRESS 1: That's nineteen out of twenty-nine. I can come up with at least ten more questions, can't you? And since September eleventh, I'm often asked them in strident, enraged, political emails. But I've gone back to responding with a swift delete. I just need to get to that quiet place.

(ACTRESS 1 *again hits the delete key, and then returns to audience.*)

ACTRESS 1: I know it's silly, but I haven't yet been able to delete Laura's screen name from my AOL address book … 29: Person you sent this to who is least likely to respond? I don't know, life is so full of surprises.

(ACTRESS 1 *sits in her chair, rocking gently, eyes closed, humming just a few bars of "Amazing Grace."*)

A VISIT TO THE ARCHIVE

BY HOLLY HUGHES

A museum guide, WOMAN, *offers original, slightly offbeat artistic interpretations of some recent acquisitions by a university library.*

SCENE
The library archives

TIME
The present

WOMAN: Welcome, welcome everyone. I would like to share with you two of the most recent additions to the Bentley Historical Library. These acquisitions are the work of Marshall Fredericks, a renowned Michigan sculptor who is sadly, dead. But of course Mr. Fredericks's masterpieces are eternal!

Who can forget his baboon series? Baboon 1, 2, 3, 4, 5, baby baboon, baboon fountain, baboon playing a mandolin, and everyone's favorite, baboon playing a ham. And his works such as Acrobat clown, circus clown, clown musicians, juggler clown and the majestic lovesick clown — these are images familiar to anyone with even a rudimentary art history background.

Is it any wonder that in 1948 our University commissioned Fredericks to create bas reliefs for the new Literature Science and the

Arts Building? Is it any surprise that when The University asked Mr. Fredericks to represent student life he presented us with a series of semi-clothed but very buff Greeks, native Americans, assorted small woodland creatures, the occasional oxen and of course, an assortment of baboons, which he claimed, were just for fun?

But the tour de force was his bronze diptych, "Dreams of a Young Man" and "Dreams of a Young Girl."

Some have criticized these extraordinary images as sexist. I would suggest that rather than viewing these works through today's gender norms, we appreciate them as historically accurate depictions of an earlier and simpler time.

In the "Dreams of a Young Man," we see a young man, reclining on his stomach. While recent critics have suggested that there is something less than manly about the young man, and that the way he appears to be smirking even as he eagerly thrusts his buttocks upwards calls into question the nature of his dream. However, there is no indication that the man who gave us such extraordinary tributes to heterosexuality as "Lovesick Clown" had any homoerotic intentions.

The dreamer is topped by a series of abstracted shapes. Experts agree the shapes clearly refer to a seafood appetizer, but disagree as to whether the dreamer is covered with a blanket of fried calamari or is dreaming in the shadow of a giant shrimp cocktail. On top of this mysterious seafood topping, two tall and majestic schooners are in full sail. Whoosh!

In the accompanying image, we see a scene of pioneer life typical of South East Michigan in 1948. A late model Conestoga wagon is in the background; from the size of the wheels one can speculate this was a really souped-up model favored by students. On Saturday nights Conestogas raced up and down State Street, sometimes at speeds of two or three miles an hour! There are a lot of farm animals in the scene, again a testimony to Mr. Fredericks's concern for historical accuracy. The sheep and oxen seem to be looking at their feet with dismay. Perhaps this is because they lack legs. The hooves seem to be directly attached to the bodies. The scene is remarkable for its absence of either baboons or clowns, rare in a Mr. Fredericks's work; again, we can only speculate what the artist intended.

In the foreground we see a tender scene of family life. Like most post-war female students, the girl sports a Holly Hobby–style bonnet and a skirt that resembles the Liberty Bell. One child is standing behind her, and appears to hate his father. The smaller child dangles off the mother's arms, and she is considering whether she should just let him fall. We can see what she is thinking—it's grass, it's not that far, would I go to jail?

Meanwhile, his father is wearing a nice set of boots, but no pants. Careful attention is paid to the boxer briefs. The torsos of both male and female figures are covered with a fabric that is either transparent, non-existent or at least very wet. The young man's six pack is lovingly described by the sculptor.

However, the young girl, like the oxen and the sheep, fails to meet our gaze. Perhaps her contact lens has popped out or her Prozac has stopped working. Yet her breasts are still optimistic. Almost cheeky. In fact, as we look at the sculpture we notice her breasts are very close to her cheeks, it is only then we realize the breasts are actually moving, they are blasting up and out of the sculpture and as they do, they seem to bid us farewell.

WAITING

BY LISA SOLAND

CINDY *is a 21-year-old college student who is sexually active: youthful in age and in her level of wisdom. Talks with a perky, rhythmic stream of consciousness. At rise, an older woman,* LINDA, *is waiting to use the bathroom.*

SCENE
The "waiting room" outside a university lecture hall

TIME
The present

CINDY: (*Enters and crosses to* LINDA.) You waiting? (LINDA *nods.*) Oh. OK. (CINDY *steps into line close behind* LINDA *and appears uncomfortable. A long silence as* CINDY *and* LINDA *wait.*) I'm usually not this impatient. It's just that I'm getting a urinary track infection and when I get those it hurts to wait. I mean, really hurts. I'm very sorry.

(*Continuing.*)

I also don't think very clearly when I'm in this kind of pain. I mean, it's an icky kind of pain. (Beat.) I shouldn't have waited this long to try to find a bathroom. I shouldn't have waited this long to see a doctor. (Quickly and loudly.) God, what is taking this woman so freakin' long? What's up with that? Why can't women just pee and get the hell on with their lives.

(*We hear the toilet flush from inside the woman's bathroom. Quickly covering her own mouth with her hand.*)

Oh God, she probably heard me. (*Beat.*) That's another symptom of an approaching urinary track infection—I have no control over my mouth either. (*Loudly, as if to woman in bathroom.*) Just have to pee, that's all. Just have to pee. (*Beat.*) The last time I got one of these, I was nearly hospitalized 'cause I waited too long to go to the doctor. I was trying to heal it "homeopathically." With cranberry juice. That's what they tell you to do. I drank so much freakin' cranberry juice I developed sores on the inside of my upper lip from the acid. Who would have known. Too much of a good thing. Never again. 'Course I say never again and here I am. (*Beat.*) It was on Valentine's day. My friend, Eric, finally took me to campus emergency 'cause I couldn't physically drive, or stand up straight, for that matter. My boyfriend at the time, was out with his mother, so he said. (*Beat.*) They I-V'd me and everything. My white blood count was sky high and they told me I had a kidney infection and it was bad. (*Thinking back.*) They scolded me. Do you believe it?! A 21-year-old woman and they're talking to me as if I'm some kind of kid. (*Beat.*) They asked me if I was a dance major and I said "no." I guess dancers get them because of the tights they gotta wear. I said, "No, just starting another relationship." (*To self.*) Just starting another relationship. (*Beat.*) I get them when I start sleeping with a new partner. I guess my body isn't used to it or something and I get them, but he finally showed up. (*Beat.*) My boyfriend. (*Explaining.*) The one at the time. (*Continuing, with a pleasant memory.*) And he had this big ol' heart-shaped box of Lady Godiva chocolates and I was starved, so we sat there and ate them together while the nurse came in and out poking me. And he kept telling me all these stupid jokes I had already heard a million times. (*Beat.*) From him. (*Beat.*) I mean, what's up with that?! (*Beat.*) It's like they don't even remember they told you them and it makes me feel like I could be anybody. Just anybody lying there in the emergency room. (*Beat.*) I tried to laugh but I kept thinking, "This isn't funny. Why does he keep trying to make me laugh?" (*Beat.*) Very painful. I get them all the time. It sucks really. I don't know what's up with that. (*Beat.*) They tell you if you pee just before you have sex, or just after sex, that that will take care of the problem. I guess it's some sort of "healthy preparation," but it doesn't work. It doesn't work. I've tried it. I've tried everything.

(*Blackout.*)

WAR OF NERVES
BY STEPHEN FIFE

Rock music playing. MELANIE, *26, sits alone, drinking a beer from the bottle.* SHE *wears tight jeans and a close-fitting top.* SHE *bobs her head in time to the music, glancing around, very coolly aloof, self-contained. Then* SHE *turns and speaks to the audience.*

SCENE
A downtown café

TIME
The present

MELANIE: Waiting is for geeks. It's for jerks. It's for people who are out of the flow, out of the mainstream, for people who don't know what their goals are or don't have any goals, who have time on their hands, time to just sit on their asses and *wait.* That is not me ... Oh no ... I would never do that, forget it, giving some perfect stranger that kind of power over me? I don't think so. My boss at the office, that's different. He knows that even when I get him coffee, he'd better say "Thanks."

(SHE *takes a slug of beer.*)

No, someone who sits there alone, who sits at a table alone, that's what I'm not, even if that's what I'm doing right now ... or what I appear to be doing ... But I have a purpose ... that's what sets me apart ...

(SHE *takes a long drink of beer. Pause.* SHE *looks SL, then looks down at her watch.*)

He'll be here in ... five to six minutes. An absolute sure thing. He's been coming like clockwork for almost three weeks. I didn't notice him at first, I'm always sitting with Janet, my best friend, she's great, you know, one of those people you can say anything to, your most personal, intimate secrets, she would never talk ... They could put her in one of those Vincent Price rooms, where the walls start closing in on you, before she'd tell any secrets she'd be squashed like a grape ... Anyway, Janet and I, we're talking and drinking, drinking and talking, you know, my boss, her boss, the guys in the mailroom, yadda, yadda, yadda ... Then one night two weeks ago I saw him. Him. The guy. At least I think it's the guy ... just standing over there at the bar, all alone, by himself, but not looking lonely or strange, not looking weird or out of place, not trying to look cool or giving every woman the eye ... just being himself. You know? That really got to me, because I'm so sick of people trying to be someone else, something they aren't, or trying to convince you that you should be impressed ... But this guy just was who he was, I could tell right away, he just *was*. And I really liked that.

(SHE *takes another slug of beer, then suddenly stands.*)

Jesus, where should I sit, table or bar? One person at a table is so pathetic, but the bar—What do you do with your hands? That's the problem. One hand goes on your beer, but the other ... It makes me wanna take up smoking again. Really badly. I mean, this guy I was with made me kick it, well he didn't "make me," but he said it was a dealbreaker, and he had the best chin . . . God! But I kicked it once before, right? And there's a machine right over there . . .

(SHE *starts walking Stage Left, then stops. Pause.*)

I don't know. A woman by herself at a bar, surrounded by a cloud of smoke . . . And then he's used to seeing me at a table. We have a routine.

(SHE *walks back to the table and sits. Pause.*)

So anyway, Janet told me that night, "That guy's been coming here for a week, throwin' you these real heavy glances." "Bullshit he has!" I said back to her and gave her a smack. But just at that moment his head turned: he had these real heavy-lidded eyes, like Robert Mitchum—who is my favorite actor of all time, even in black-and-white—I would tumble for him in a heartbeat . . . Anyway, his eyes made contact with mine and I felt something . . . It went up and down my spine, like in some weird sci-fi flick, it felt like the nerve-endings jumped out of our bodies and met in mid-air, twisting and coiling around each other into this tight, slimy knot, while people danced and talked all around.

(SHE *looks down at her watch.*)

He should be here right now . . . He should be walking in that door any second. I'm really pissed that Janet isn't here with me, I mean what kind of friend acts like that? "I can't take it anymore," she tells me, "you won't say hello, and you won't let me say hello for you." Well, what does she think it's been like for me, with those nerve-endings twitching outside my body? But I'm the kind of person who doesn't like to be pushed, so I've been pulling back for two weeks now, and it's killing me. Tearing me up inside, my appetite has been for shit, I can't even stomach a Mallomar, and sleep—yeah. Just forget about sleep. But I don't wanna do something unless I'm *sure* that I wanna do it. And I haven't been sure. Not 'til tonight. (SHE *looks at her watch.*)

And now he's late, I don't believe this, the shithead... He's never been late before... He's probably doing this on purpose, he knows what tonight is, and he's trying to push me... (SHE *takes a long slug of beer.*) What if something's happened? What if he's been in an accident, a bus ran him over, or maybe one of those big delivery vans, they come shooting around a corner like bats out of hell, and then—He could be lying in a hospital somewhere maybe in a coma, maybe near death, or in a great deal of pain... and I don't even know how to find him, I don't even know the guy's name... Or maybe he just isn't coming. Maybe he went off to a party, or to another bar with a bunch of the guys, he's tellin' funny stories about me... "Yeah, this chick, this babe, this babola"—I know how guys talk—"I hung out at this bar for a few weeks, I got her all hot and bothered, she's probably chewin' her panties right now..." We'll see about that.

(MELANIE *jumps up from the table, takes two strides, stops.*)

God, I hate Janet, I really do, I'll never forgive her...

(*Pause:* SHE *takes a step back toward the table.*)

I gotta have a cigarette, Jesus, or I'm gonna die...

(SHE *moves swiftly SL, then stops in her tracks.*)

Oh my God! He's here, he's really here! What am I gonna do?

WHEN GRACE COMES IN
BY HEATHER MCDONALD

The wife of a Senator, MARGARET GRACE BRAXTON, *42, recounts the time she either fell or jumped in front of a moving vehicle while holding her young infant.*

SCENE
The Braxton home

TIME
The present

MARGARET: One time, when you were very little, a baby, you still had that sweet babyhead smell, and this one time, just past dawn, I ran out of diapers...I'd been up off and on all night alone with you, you were cutting teeth or colicky or something, and your Dad was away, Bill was away campaigning or primaries or something, it being November, it always being November, and I bundled you up in a blanket and ran barefoot down the street in my bathrobe to the store to get more diapers, and when I got to the store, they were out of diapers, yes, they were out of diapers, and you were crying by then, and my breasts were leaking through the housecoat, and I held you in my arms and ran out of the store back toward the house.

Now, the way I remember what happened next and the way I told it was this—I jumped out of the way of the car to save you. To save you. But the way the driver and the two other people told it, I jumped into the way of the car. I landed on my back, oddly instinctual, protecting the baby in my arms. I don't remember my blind rage that they were out of diapers or the leap into the air while clutching my child, the screech of the car, the horn honking, the shouting of witnesses, the way they looked at me, the frazzled young mother who had momentarily gone mad and hurled herself and her baby in front of a car. Those images are faint. What I do remember with absolute clarity is lying on my back and looking up at the sky, a sky the color of disappointment. And there was a bird above me, and with every beat of its wings, I heard a whisper, worse, worse, worse, worse.

I knew then very clearly what I was up against and what I needed to do. I needed to be careful, to keep that mad mother in the stained bathrobe in check, because my job now was to take care of you because your life was in my hands and my job was to be a nice young mother.

I've never done anything like that again.

WHITE RUSSIAN
BY JOSEPH GOODRICH

Because of the dangerous nature of the country, Katja *is willing to take refuge in the town nearby.* She *is not in good health and has felt unbeautiful and unloved.* She *speaks to* Wynton, *a friend in the military.*

SCENE
A foreign country

TIME
The present

Katja: Did you know I've been married?

[Wynton: I didn't know that.]

Katja: Yes, I was. I was married for ... two years — no, I take that back. Three years. (*Pause.*) He's dead now.

[Wynton: I'm sorry.]

Katja: It was a long time ago. But thank you. (*Pause.*) He had no will, either. Worse than that, he had no volition. A certain pale charm, that was all. A very pale charm. Most people loathed him. (*Pause.*)

You see, I wasn't loved as a girl. I developed a wide-ranging set of illnesses because of this. Naturally I place the blame for this on my family. I am more sinned against than sinning in this respect. Yes, I have acted coldly — even heartlessly — but all my efforts have been directed toward health and integrity of the self. I'm still not entirely well. I'm due for a new cornea after Lent. But I have my hopes. Surely that's the important thing? (*Pause.*) I was the older, more experienced party in the relationship. Men had used me in the past, used my body for their own satisfaction. Kip nearly destroyed me. I'd sit in my room at university, with a penicillin drip in my arm, playing my Spanish guitar and singing my songs of revenge. I'd been used by everyone but never loved. I'd almost given up when Parky found me. I was growing older. I was no longer a blushing young thing. I've never been a blushing young thing, actually. I've never been beautiful. Not like other girls. Not even in the flower of youth — such as it was, my shy and secretive youth blighted with illness and neurosis and damage. But when I saw him in his light green shirt and colorful trousers, and heard him speak, and saw that he needed to love as much as I needed to *be* loved — all that was past. A *coupe de foudre* on the grand scale. He wasn't graceful, he wasn't bright, he wasn't even very handsome. He was about as weak a cup of tea as could be imagined. But he listened to my songs, he admired them, and I loved his little drawings of pandas and ponies and baby whales. He loved me. And I loved him … for a time.

WHITE RUSSIAN

BY JOSEPH GOODRICH

As a Russian émigré in this unsettled country, Adriana *is urged to leave her home and move to town where it is safer.* She *has refused vehemently, but apologizes for losing her composure. She is with* Katja, *a woman willing to relocate for safety's sake, who tries to persuade* Adriana *by plying her with alcohol.*

SCENE
A foreign country

TIME
The present

Adriana: It's not. Not really. I'm the one who's supposed to maintain the tone around here. I'm not supposed to have screaming-fuck-fits. Oh, no. That's not allowed around here. More please. (Katja *refills her glass.*) What galls me about this situation is the lack of choice. If I wanted to leave, if I chose to leave—I'd leave. But to have no choice in the matter galls me. Fact is, I don't want to leave. I want to stay here where I've always been. I'm very happy here, thank you very much. Thank you very much, indeed. More, please. (Katja *refills her glass.*) And where are we going, when we go? Has anyone addressed that question? No. Certainly not to my satisfaction. Into town, he says. All right, but where in town? And with whom? From this to—what? A tiny little house we share with some *soi-disant artiste* and his pack of yapping hounds? Greasy stoves and show tunes? Semen-stained sofas and dog-hair soup? We're not immigrants. We're émigrés. And it is here that we have settled. We have made this place our home. And I'll be damned if I'm leaving it. More, please. (KATJA *refills her glass.*) I'll be damned if I'll give all this up at the slightest hint of a little danger. Life is dangerous! We risk immolation when we step out the door! It's a truism! More, please. (KATJA *refills her glass.*) I'm going completely out on the edge of the tree. I know that. And I don't care. I am not all gentle milkiness and sweet consideration. There is within me bitter gall on this sad occasion. I go, I know not whither. I suffer now for what hath former been. 'Tis the times' plague when madmen lead the blind. More, please. (KATJA *refills her glass.*) O, for a muse of fire!... More, please.

[KATJA: Perhaps you shouldn't]

ADRIANA: You dare to bandy looks with me, you rogue? More, please. And now, Goddamnit! (KATJA *brings her the bottle.*) Thank you. The point I'm making is this, dear Katja. The films of Federico Fellini constitute for me the deepest, most touching, most inventive work the cinema has ever produced. I bow to my masters: Fellini and Del. Both are dead, and both live on. They will always be living presences in my life. Whereas everyone else is dead. Everyone else is dead. And nothing—nothing—will bring them back.

YEMAYA'S BELLY
BY QUIARA ALEGRIA HUDES

A young boy and his uncle travel from their remote village to the city where they observe a young festival dancer, YEMAYA, *dressed in a regal costume, as she performs a ritual chant.*

SCENE
An island surrounded by the ocean

TIME
Recent history

YEMAYA: (*Placing a cup before her, for collecting tips.*) For the spirits. (JELIN *and* JESUS *put some change in her cup.* YEMAYA *performs.*)

Remember me like you remember your ancestors

memory more vast than your human years

search back to the treasures in your birth

and find me there

Many of your ancestors were buried in my belly

blue eyes lie blind in my water

brown eyes lie blind in my water

in my dark water they are all the same,

the eyes of your ancestors

Do not forget me

come back to me

and I will slay your enemies

I will crusade for your comfort

I will swallow those who spite you

I will leave your enemies crying in shame

Then when death comes

you will see through the eyes of your parents

you will see through the eyes

that saw before you

you will speak through an eternal voice.

(*Touching* JESUS *with the feather on "my children."*)

My children move in broad strokes

across this mortal world

just as my tide travels the large surface of the earth

But my tide is regular

and returns to the same shores

So do the hearts of my children

return to me

to the breast of Yemaya

(*Her performance is over.* She *takes her change cup … exits.*)

YIT, NGAY (ONE, TWO)

BY MICHAEL LEW

Recently immigrated to the United States from China, JOOK *is now in her 60s, hard, stout, and curt. The war bent her sister Mei, but it broke* JOOK. *She has not forgotten the struggle to survive nor the loss of their mother.*

SCENE
Fresno, California

TIME
Late 1990s

JOOK: When the war ended, Ba Ba came home. He had served in the American Navy, and there was a G.I. bill that let the soldiers take home a war bride. He pretended that he had just met Ma Ma so he could take her with him to America. Naturally, he could not take us. How could he explain having a new bride from China and also having daughters ten and twelve years old? But he spent some time with us, a year perhaps, and those were the first times I had ever known my father. This man who had sent us money from America was a real Ba Ba like all the other girls had. But then it came time for him to leave. It was then that I decided I hated my father. This man was going to leave us again, and he was going to take our mother! What were Mei and I to do? If we were boys, maybe he would have stayed. Maybe he wouldn't dare go back to America, but we were girls and we were worthless and he wanted to start a new family. Worthless girls who survived an entire war without the protection of the men, least of all protection from him! Ma Ma was crying. She told him she would never leave us. But Ba Ba told her, "If you don't go, then they will starve. All three of you will starve! You'll live your entire life like my mother! Look at her! A spinster! Do you want to be a spinster like her? But if you come with me, we can have sons. We can send the girls money. Or someday we could even send for them." This man was taking away my mother and he was insulting my Yeen Yeen? The two women who got us through those times when our village was burning all year round! Someday send for us? I told myself I'd never go. I would never leave Yeen Yeen, who braved the war with us, hobbling on her bad knee. This man swooped down and orphaned us, and he thought that sending money would mend that? Mei doesn't remember this, but I do. Some days, I still wake up with the stench of smoke in my hair.

PLAY SOURCES AND ACKNOWLEDGMENTS

Adamson, Jo J., © 2007. *Teotwawki.* Reprinted by permission of the author. Inquiries may be directed to the author, Jo J. Adamson, 25252 Lake Wilderness Country Club Drive S.E., Maple Valley, WA 98038.

Appel, Dori, © 2001. *Lost and Found.* Reprinted by permission of the author. Contact Dori Appel, P.O. Box 1364, Ashland, OR 97520; applcart@mind.net, 541-482-2735.

Auburn, David, © 2002. *Are You Ready?* c/o the author's agent, Chris Till, Paradigm, 19 West 44 St., Suite 1410, New York, NY 10036.

Barnett, Claudia, © 2007. *Feather.* Reprinted by permission of the author. Contact Claudia Barnett at cbarnett@mtsu.edu.

Basham, Rebecca, © 2001. *Lot's Daughters.* Reprinted by permission of the playwright. Inquiries should be directed to the author at rbasham@rider.edu.

Brewer, Gaylord, © 2007. *Dog My Cats, or The Stalker Play.* Reprinted by permission of the author. Contact Gaylord Brewer at gbrewer@mtsu.edu.

Bull, Katie, © 2004. "*Message from the Driver*" from *The 29 Questions Project,* © 2004 by Katie Bull and Hillary Rollins. Inquiries concerning all rights should be directed to Ms. Bull's website, www.katiebull.com.

Callaghan, Sheila, © 2006. *Dead City.* Reprinted by permission of the author. Inquiries should be directed to the Mark Christian Subias Agency, 331 West 57th Street, No. 462 New York, NY 10019, marksubias@earthlink.net.

Cruz, Nilo, © 2004. *Night Train to Bolivia.* Reprinted by permission of the author. Inquiries concerning all rights should be directed to the Peregrine Whittlesey Agency, 345 East 80th St., New York, NY 10021.

Davis, Lenning A. Jr., © 2000. *The Dance.* Reprinted by permission of the author. Contact Lenning Davis, 103 Granite Ave., Canaan, CT 06018.

Fife, Stephen, © 2002. *Lola's Vision*. Reprinted by permission of the author. Please direct all inquiries to the author at slfife@aol.com or to P.O. Box 5425, Santa Monica, CA 90409.

Fife, Stephen, © 2004. *War of Nerves.* Reprinted by permission of the author. Please direct all inquiries to the author at slfife@aol.com or to P.O. Box 5425, Santa Monica, CA 90409.

Fornes, Maria Irene, © 2000, 2007. *Enter the Night.* All inquiries should be directed to the author's agent, Morgan Jenness, Abrams Artists Agency, 275 Seventh Ave., 26th Floor, New York, NY 10001.

Gibson, William, © 2003. *Golda's Balcony*. Reprinted by permission of the author. Please direct inquiries to the Lantz Office, 200 W. 57th St., New York, NY 10019.

Goodrich, Joseph, © 2004. *White Russian*. Reprinted by permission of the author. All inquiries regarding performance rights should be addressed to Joseph Goodrich, 1738 University Ave., St. Paul, MN 55104.

Greenidge, Kirsten, © 2004. *Sans-Culottes in the Promised Land*. c/o the Bret Adams, Ltd., 448 W. 44th St., New York, NY 10036, Attn: Bruce Ostler.

Groff, Rinne, © 2003. *Orange Lemon Egg Canary*. All inquiries should be addressed to the William Morris Agency, 1325 Ave. of the Americas, New York, NY, Attn: Val Day.

Grote, Jason, © 2004. *Kawaisoo (The Pity of Things)*. Reprinted by permission of the author. All inquiries regarding performing rights should be addressed to Jason Grote, 423 Clermont Ave., #1, Brooklyn, NY 11238.

Guirgis, Stephen Adly, © 2001, 2003. *"Jesus Hopped the A Train"* from *Our Lady of 121st Street, Jesus Hopped the A Train and in Arabia, We's All Be Kings.* Reprinted by permission of Faber and Faber, Inc., an affiliate of Farrar, Straus, and Giroux, LLC.

Haines, Laurel, © 2003. *The Dianalogues*. Caution Notice: All Rights Reserved. Professionals and amateurs are hereby warned that this play is subject to a royalty. It is fully protected under the copyright laws of the United States of America, British Commonwealth, including Canada, and all other countries of the Copyright Union. All rights, including professional, amateur, motion picture, recitation, lecturing, public reading, radio and television broadcasting,

Kennicott, Leigh, © 2007. *Scenes From an Unfinished Life*. Reprinted by permission of the author. Contact: myhecuba@sbcglobal.net.

Knox, Paul, © 2004. *Kalighat*. Reprinted by permission of the author. All inquiries should be directed to the author, c/o New York Theatre Experience, PO Box 1606, Murray Hill Station, New York, NY 10156, or through the Circle East Theatre, www.circleeast.com.

Kochanski, Kerri, © 2002. *Communicating Through the Sunset*. Reprinted by permission of the author. Please direct inquiries to the author at kerrikochanski@optionline.net.

LaBute, Neil, © 2004. *Fat Pig*. Reprinted by permission of Faber and Faber, Inc., an affiliate of Farrar, Straus and Griroux, LLC.

LaBute, Neil, © 2003. *The Mercy Seat*. Reprinted by permission of Faber and Faber, Inc., an affiliate of Farrar, Straus and Giroux, LLC.

LaBute, Neil, © 2006. *Some Girl(s)*. Reprinted by permission of Faber and Faber, Inc., an affiliate of Farrar, Straus and Giroux, LLC.

Lee, Young Jean, © 2006. *Songs of the Dragons Flying to Heaven*. Reprinted by permission of the author. Inquiries should be directed to the author's agent Val Day at the William Morris Agency, vday@wma.com.

Lew, Michael, © 2003. *Yit, Ngay (One, Two)*. Reprinted by permission of the author. Amateurs and professional are hereby warned that *Yit, Ngay (One, Two)* is fully protected by copyright law and is subject to royalty. All rights in all current and future media are strictly reserved. No part of this work may be used for any purpose without the author's consent. All inquiries concerning the use of this work should be addressed to the author. By email: michael.lew@aya.yale.edu. By phone: 646-942-7763. by mail: Michael Lew, c/o The New York Theatre Experience, Inc., P.O. Box 1606 Murray Hill Station, New York, NY 10156. Full text available in *Plays and Playwrights* 2006 (The New York Theatre Experience, Inc.; Martin Denton, ed.).

Lipkin, Joan, © 2006. *Small Domestic Acts*. Reprinted by permission of the author. Inquiries should be directed to the author at jlipkin@aol.com.

Lunch, Lydia, © 2006. *Johnny Behind the Deuce*. Reprinted by permission of the author. Contact Tom Garretson at info@wildstarworld.com.

Lunch, Lydia, © 2006. *Real Pornography*. Reprinted by permission of the author. Contact Tom Garretson at info@wildstarworld.com.

Reingold, Jacquelyn, © 2003. *String Fever*. Reprinted by permission of the author. For performance rights to *String Fever*, contact Dramatists Play Service, 440 Park Avenue South, New York, NY 10016.

Rifkin, June, © 1992, 2007. *Seperation Anxiety*. Reprinted by permission of the author. All inquiries can be directed to the author, junerifkin@aol.com or June Rifkin, c/o Peter Rubie Literary Agency, 240 W. 35th St., Suite 500, New York, NY 10001.

Rimmer, David, © 2006. *New York*. Reprinted by permission of the author. Direct inquiries to the author, rimmersandhaus@aol.com, or David Rimmer, 11 East 78th St., 4A, New York, NY 10021, or 212-794-2430.

Rollins, Hillary, © 2001. *The 29 Questions Project*. Reprinted by permission of the author. Inquiries to h.d.rollins@verizon.net.

Schisgal, Murray, *The Empty Stage*. Reprinted by permission of the author. All inquiries should be directed to A.B. Greene & Co., 101 Park Ave., New York, NY 10178.

Schrum, Stephen A., © 2006. *Dog Assassin*. Reprinted by permission of the author. Please direct inquiries to the author, steveschrum@yahoo.com.

Shuman, Bob, © 2007. *Soul Healing*. Reprinted by permission of the author. Please direct inquires to the author c/o Marit Literary Agency; bobjshuman@gmail.com.

Simpatico, David, © 2006. *The Secret of Life*. Reprinted by permission of the author (to Jane and Janey and John). Please direct inquiries to the author, davidsimpatico@yahoo.com.

Smith, Anna Deavere, © 2003. *House Arrest and Piano: Two Plays*. Used by permission of Ancho Books, a division of Random House, Inc.

Soland, Lisa, © 2001. *The Rebirth*. Reprinted by permission of the author. Please direct inquiries to the author, lisasoland@aol.com, or Lisa Soland, PO Box 33081, Granada Hills, CA 91394.

Soland, Lisa, © 2002. *Waiting*. Reprinted by permission of the author. Please direct inquiries to the author, lisasoland@aol.com, or Lisa Soland, PO Box 33081, Granada Hills, CA 91394.

Stokley, Margie, © 2005. *Elephant*. Reprinted by permission of the author. All inquiries should be directed to the author, stokley@aol.com, or margie@andhowtheater.com.

Swedeen, Staci, © 2006. *Dottie*. Reprinted by permission of the author. Please direct inquiries to Elaine Devlin Literary Agency, c/o Plus Entertainment, 20 West 23 St., 3rd Floor, New York, NY 10010, or to the author, staciswede@aol.com or www.staciswedeen.com

Temperley, Stephen, © 2005. *Souvenir*. Reprinted by permission of the author. Inquiries may be directed to the author, temperly@earthling.net.

Urban, Ken, © 2001. *Halo*. Reprinted by permission of the author. All inquiries concerning production or publication rights or requests to reprint any portion of the use of this work should be directed to the author, Ken Urban, c/o The Committee Theatre Co., PO Box 1151, Midtown Station, New York, NY 10018.

Utterback, Neal, © 2004. *Second*. Reprinted by permission of the author. Please direct all inquiries to the author, nealau@yahoo.com.

Warnock, Kathleen, © 2005. *Rock the Line*. Reprinted by permission of the author. Direct inquiries to the author, kwnyc@yahoo.com; order copies of *Rock the Line* from www.unitedstages.com.

Wilson, August, © 2003. *Gem of the Ocean*. The Play is published by and reprinted with the permission of Theatre Communication Group, 520 Eighth Avenue, New York, NY 10018.

Wright, Craig, © 2002. *Orange Flower Water*. Reprinted by permission of Abrams Artists Agency on behalf of the Author, © 2004. Contact Beth Blickers, Abrams Artists Agency, 275 Seventh Ave., 26th Floor, New York, NY 10001.

Wyatt, Randy, © 2004. *The Ghost Moments*. Reprinted by permission of the author. All inquiries may be directed to the author at thecove@gmail.com.

Yaged, Kim, © 2006. *Hypocrites & Strippers*. Reprinted by permission of the author. Please direct inquiries to the author, kyaged@gmail.com.

Yankowitz, Susan, © 2007. *The Ludicrous Trial of Mr. P.* Reprinted by permission of the author. Full script available from the author at 205 W. 89th St., #8F, New York, NY 10024 or contact: syankowitz@aol.com or www.susanyankowitz.com

Zwerling, Phil, © 2005. *The Face in the Mirror*. Reprinted by permission of the author, assistant professor of English at University of Texax Pan American, pzwerling@utpa.edu.

Additionally, the editors would like to thank the extraordinary writers who so graciously allowed their work to be used in this volume, as well as: Applause Books, Bret Adams, Dennis Aspland, Beth Blickers, Justin Cavin, Clare Cerullo, Margie Connor, June Clark, Val Day, Martin and Rochelle Denton, Lisa Drew, Kenneth Ferrone, Carol Flannery, Victoria Fox, Pam Green, Peter Hagan, Meg Hammer, Patrick Herold, Morgan Jenness, Dee Josephson, Robert Lantz, Bernadette Malavarca, Michael Messina, Nancy Nelson and Randy Lanchner, Jonathan Lomma, Ivy McDaniel, New York Theatre Experience, Janet Nohavec, Jiwon Park, Kathleen Peirce, Eric Price, Hillary Rollins, Joseph Rosswog, Peter Rubie, Betty Russo, Chris Till, Karen Schimmel, Zachary Schisgal, Marit Shuman, the Shuman and Nolan families, Rita Battat-Silverman and Steve Silverman, Arthur Stanley, Ursinus College, Kathleen Warnock, Peregrine Whittlesey, Laura Wildman, Gary Winter, and Belinda Yong.

THE EDITORS

Joyce E. Henry is professor emirata of Theatre and Communication Studies at Ursinus College. She is the editor of *The Wisdom of Shakespeare* and author of *Beat the Bard*. She lives in Collegeville, Pennsylvania.

Rebecca Dunn Jaroff is assistant professor of English at Ursinus College where she teaches American literature, drama, and journalism. She is the author of several essays on nineteenth-century American women playwrights. She lives in Conshohocken, Pennsylvania.

Bob Shuman is the owner of Marit Literary Agency (affiliated with the Peter Rubie Literary Agency) in New York. He is an editor, playwright, college professor, and co-author of *Simply Elegant Flowers with Michael George*. A Fellow of the Lark Theatre Company, Bob received Hunter College's Irv Zarkower Award for excellence in playwriting. He lives in New York City.